# Remember This?

*People, Things and Events*
FROM **1963** TO THE **PRESENT DAY**

UK EDITION

# Rewind, Replay, Remember

What can you remember before you turned six? If you're like most of us, not much: the comforting smell of a blanket or the rough texture of a sweater, perhaps. A mental snapshot of a parent arriving home late at night. A tingle of delight or the shadow of sorrow.

But as we grow out of childhood, our autobiographical and episodic memories – they're the ones hitched to significant events such as birthdays or leaving school – are created and filed more effectively, enabling us to piece them together at a later date. And the more we revisit those memories, the less likely we are to lose the key that unlocks them.

These fragments are assembled into a more-or-less coherent account of our lives – the one we tell ourselves, our friends, our relatives. And while this one-of-a-kind biopic loses a little definition over the years, some episodes remain in glorious technicolour – although it's often the most embarrassing incidents!

But this is one movie that's never quite complete. Have you ever had a memory spring back unbidden, triggered by something seemingly unrelated? This book is an attempt to discover those forgotten scenes using the events, sounds, and faces linked to the milestones in your life.

It's time to blow off the cobwebs and see how much you can remember!

# It Happened in 1963

The biggest event in the year is one that didn't make the front pages: you were born! Here are some of the national stories that people were talking about.

✦ Beeching Report calls for huge cuts in UK rail network
✦ Steam train Flying Scotsman makes last London to Edinburgh trip
✦ President De Gaulle vetoes UK joining the EEC
✦ Armed gang steals £2.6m from night mail train (right)
✦ Macmillan resigns; Alec Douglas-Home becomes prime minister
✦ £13m Dartford Tunnel linking Essex and Kent opens
✦ Kenya declares independence from Britain
✦ UK, US and USSR sign treaty banning all nuclear tests
✦ Labour Party leader Hugh Gaitskell dies suddenly at 56
✦ Midlands town Dudley hit by race riots
✦ Beatlemania sweeps UK; screaming fans greet Fab Four on tour
✦ Barbie's British rival fashion-doll Sindy goes on sale
✦ First episode of sci-fi series Dr Who airs on BBC TV
✦ Last CND Aldermaston to London march takes place
✦ Spurs win Cup Winners' Cup, first UK team to win European trophy
✦ Sex, spies and politics scandal Profumo Affair rocks the nation
✦ Film musical Summer Holiday starring Cliff Richard released
✦ David Lean's epic Lawrence of Arabia wins Best Picture Oscar
✦ Edward Craven-Walker invents the decade's iconic Lava lamp
✦ The Beatles release their debut album Please Please Me

*Born this year:*
⚬ Olympic ski-jumper Eddie 'The Eagle' Edwards born in Cheltenham
⚬ Actress and author Meera Syal born in Wolverhampton
⚬ England and Arsenal goalkeeper David Seaman born in Rotherham

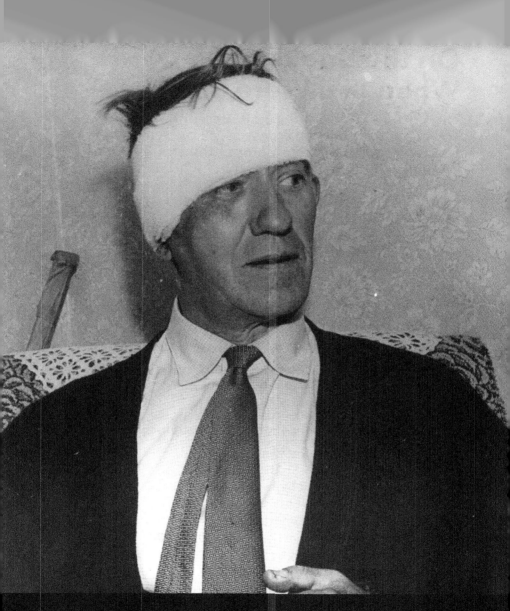

Who wielded the cosh that felled train driver Jack Mills during The Great Train Robbery of 1963? Mills is seen above; a bandage was applied by the robbers after he fell. The culprit certainly derailed the gang's plans for a 'gentleman robbery'. But few know who it was, and nobody's telling – or if they are, it's not necessarily the truth. A 2012 deathbed confession from robber Jim Hussey is rubbished by Mills' son, who reports that his father told him the name of the assailant, though he won't say who that is. He takes pride in his father's actions during the robbery but is sure the attack led to his father's early death from leukaemia at the age of 64.

# On the Bookshelf When You Were Small

The books of our childhood linger long in the memory. These are the children's classics, all published in your first ten years. Do you remember the stories? What about the covers?

| | |
|---|---|
| 1963 | The Secret Passage by Nina Bawden |
| 1963 | Stig of the Dump by Clive King |
| 1963 | Where the Wild Things Are by Maurice Sendak |
| 1964 | On the Run by Nina Bawden |
| 1964 | Flat Stanley by Jeff Brown |
| 1964 | Charlie and the Chocolate Factory by Roald Dahl |
| 1964 | **Chitty-Chitty-Bang-Bang by Ian Fleming** <br> It was adapted for film four years after Fleming's death – produced by Albert R Broccoli, co-written by Roald Dahl. |
| 1965 | Over Sea, Under Stone by Susan Cooper |
| 1966 | The Witch's Daughter by Nina Bawden |
| 1966 | **The Magic Finger by Roald Dahl** <br> Originally titled The Almost Ducks, publication in the US was delayed over fears of offending the gun lobby. |
| 1967 | The Owl Service by Alan Garner |
| 1967 | The Outsiders by SE Hinton |
| 1967 | Brown Bear, What Do You See? by Bill Martin Jr |
| 1968 | The Wombles by Elisabeth Beresford |
| 1968 | The Iron Man by Ted Hughes |
| 1968 | The Tiger Who Came to Tea by Judith Kerr |
| 1968 | Elmer the Elephant by David McKee |
| 1968 | The Pigman by Paul Zindel |
| 1969 | **The Very Hungry Caterpillar by Eric Carle** <br> Began life as A Week With Willi the Worm, the story of a bookworm, but Carle's publisher requested a caterpillar. |
| 1970 | **Are You There, God? It's Me, Margaret by Judy Blume** <br> Challenged and banned due to the discussion of menstruation, puberty, pornography, and religion. |
| 1970 | Fantastic Mr Fox by Roald Dahl |
| 1971 | Mr. Tickle by Roger Hargreaves |
| 1972 | Freaky Friday by Mary Rodgers |

# Around the World in Your Birth Year

Here are the events from abroad that were big enough to make news at home in the year you were born. And you won't remember any of them!

✦ Vajont Dam landslide kills over 2,000 in northern Italy
✦ Organisation of African Unity formed to support decolonisation
✦ US embargo on trade and travel devastates Cuban economy
✦ Soviet cosmonaut Valentina Tereshkova is first woman in space
✦ British double agent Kim Philby given asylum in Moscow
✦ Icelandic undersea eruption creates new island of Surtsey
✦ Nelson Mandela charged with plot to overthrow government
✦ JFK's 'Ich bin ein Berliner' speech pledges US-German solidarity
✦ Monk's suicide by fire over South Vietnam's Buddhist persecution
✦ American poet Sylvia Plath commits suicide in London
✦ Zanzibar gains independence from Britain
✦ Earthquake levels Skopje in Yugoslavia, over 1,000 killed
✦ US president John F Kennedy assassinated in Dallas, Texas
✦ Luxury sports-car maker Lamborghini founded in Bologna, Italy
✦ Lyndon B Johnson sworn in as 36th US president
✦ Martin Luther King's 'I have a dream' speech calls for equality
✦ Tito named life president of Yugoslavian socialist republic
✦ Alfred Hitchcock's avian thriller The Birds released in USA

*Born this year:*
⚔ Chess champ Garry Kasparov born in Baku, Azerbaijan
⚔ US basketball giant Michael Jordan born in New York
⚔ Chat-show host Graham Norton born in Clondalkin, Ireland
⚔ Friends actress Lisa Kudrow born in Encino, California

# Boys' Names When You Were Born

Stuck for a name in the early 20th century? The answer was simple: use your own. Will nobody think of the genealogists? Here are the most popular names in England and Wales in 1963.

**David**
David has wrestled control of the top spot from John, and he'll keep it for twenty years.

John
Stephen
Michael
Peter
Robert
Paul
Alan
Christopher
Richard
Anthony
Andrew
Ian
James
William
Philip
Brian
Keith
Graham

**Rising and falling stars:**
Farewell Bernard, Frank, Norman, Leonard, Lawrence and Clifford. Give a big Top 100 welcome to Jeremy, Julian and all the G's: Gerard, Garry, Gareth and Gregory and Glenn.

*A note about other parts of the UK:*
Baby name data isn't available until 1974 for Scotland and the turn of the century for Northern Ireland. How different are they? In the mid-seventies around a third of Scotland's Top 100 boys' names weren't in the English and Welsh equivalent – but the highest ranked of these was Gordon at number 30. By 2019, Scotland-only names ranked 4th (Harris), 7th (Lewis), 18th (Brodie), 22nd (Finlay) and more.

# Girls' Names When You Were Born

Some parents pick names that are already popular. Others try to pick something more unusual – only to find out a few years later that thousands had the same idea.

**Susan**
After thirty years, Susan takes the top spot from Margaret.
Linda
Christine
Margaret
Janet
Patricia
Carol
Elizabeth
Mary
Anne
Ann
Jane
Jacqueline
Barbara
Sandra
Gillian
Pauline
Elaine
Lesley
Angela
Pamela
Helen
Jennifer
Valerie
**Jean**
Slides from the Top 100 are usually gentle. But not for Jean: by the sixties, she was gone.

**Rising and falling stars:**
A quarter of names in this Top 100 haven't been seen since, including Rita, Geraldine and Doreen. Taking their place are names such as Gail, Dawn, Anna, Fiona and Beverley.

# Things People Did When You Were Growing Up...

...that hardly anyone does now. Some of these we remember fondly; others are best left in the past!

+ Use a mangle
+ **Use an outside toilet**
  Slum clearances and grants saw the end of most outside toilets, although in 2010 around 40,000 properties still had one.

+ Take the trolley bus to school
+ Fetch coal from the cellar
+ Wear a hat to work
+ **Use a coal tar vaporizer**
  A coal tar inhaler or vaporizer – probably made by Wright's, with the matching liquid – seemed like a good idea for treating whooping cough. It wasn't. A 1930s example held by the National Trust has a simple caption: 'This is poisonous.'

+ Travel without a seatbelt
+ **Rent a TV**
  When tellies cost a fortune (and frequently broke), renting a TV made sense. Where to go? Radio Rentals, who promised, 'You'll be glued to our sets, not stuck with them!'

+ **Wear a housecoat**
  Who can think of a housecoat and curlers without remembering Coronation Street's Hilda Ogden?

+ Scrub your doorstep
+ Creosote the fence (banned for DIY in 2003)
+ **Smoke a pipe**
  Stephen Fry was the last Pipe Smoker of the Year, in 2003.

+ **Spank (or be spanked)**
  Corporal punishment ended in most schools in 1986. It is illegal in Scottish and Welsh homes, but not in England or N. Ireland.

+ Pay the Pools collector
+ Build a soapcart
+ **Write a letter**
  Royal Mail still handles 10 billion letters each year but very few are handwritten. More than a fifth of UK children have never received a letter.

# Old-fashioned Games

In a pre-digital age, boardgames ruled. Many of these predate you buy decades, centuries or more but still played; others gather dust in attics and charity shops.

| | |
|---|---|
| 1928 | Escalado |
| 1934 | Sorry! |
| 1935 | **Monopoly** |

The origins of this stalwart lie with The Landlord's Game, an education tool patented in 1904 by Elizabeth Magie. (The anti-monopoly version – Prosperity – didn't catch on.) It was the first game to feature a never-ending path rather than a fixed start and finish.

| | |
|---|---|
| 1938 | Buccaneer |
| 1938 | Scrabble |
| 1935 | Whot! |
| 1947 | Subbuteo |
| 1949 | **Cluedo** |

Cluedo, or Clue as it is known in the USA, introduced us to a host of shady country house characters and a selection of murder weapons. For years those included a piece of genuine lead pipe – thankfully replaced on health grounds.

| | |
|---|---|
| 1925 | Dover Patrol |
| 1851 | **Happy Families** |

The original and much-copied Happy Families card game was launched for the Great Exhibition in 1851. For 20th Century children, Happy Families also means the million-selling book series by Allan Ahlberg, based loosely on the card game, which in turn inspired a BBC series.

| | |
|---|---|
| 1889 | **Tiddlywinks** |

Trademarked as Tiddledy-Winks by Joseph Fincher, this much-maligned game has nevertheless found fans at elite universities, spawned countless spin-offs and rule variations (known in Tiddlywink parlance as 'perversions').

| | |
|---|---|
| 1896 | Ludo |
| 1892 | Chinese Chequers |
| 1938 | Totopoly |
| Ancient Egypt | Mancala |

# Things People Do Now...

...that were virtually unknown when you were young. How many of these habits are part of your routine or even second nature these days? Do you remember the first time?

+ Shop on Sunday (made possible in England and Wales in 1994)
+ Microwave a curry
+ **Leave a voicemail**
  At least you'll never have to change the cassette again!
+ **Watch last night's TV**
  Nowadays, you don't have to remember to set the VCR (and get a small child to help you do it). BBC iPlayer was the UK's first on-demand, streaming service, launched in 2007.

+ Strim grass
+ Change a fitted sheet
+ Recharge your toothbrush
+ Order a takeaway meal... to be delivered
+ Delete a photo
+ **Fit a disposable nappy**
  The first disposable 'napkins' went on sale in 1949 as two-part Paddis, invented by Valerie Hunter Gordon.

+ Eat an avocado
+ Use Google
+ Take a shower
+ **Make a video call (right)**
+ Buy a cheap flight
+ **Floss your teeth**
  Not a flosser? Take heart from a 2016 US research review: evidence for its benefit is very weak, and official advice to floss was dropped. Poking around with those pesky interdental brushes is how you should be spending your time (and money).

+ Pressure wash your patio
+ **Stick a self-adhesive stamp**
  You can probably still remember the taste of stamp glue, even though the sticky versions were introduced in 1993.

+ Answer an email (or send it to spam)
+ **Use a duvet**
  Sir Terence Conran is credited with finally persuading Brits to ditch the blankets when he introduced duvets in his Habitat stores in the sixties.

*Mary Evans / Everett Collection*

Zoom, Skype, FaceTime and more: if you weren't making face-to-face calls before the lockdowns of 2020, that's probably when you made your first. But it has taken 50 years to catch on and for technology to catch up: shown above is AT&T's PicturePhone, demonstrated in 1964 at New York's World's Fair. (The cost didn't help: renting a pair of devices for three minutes cost

# Popular Food from the 1950s

Rationing was thankfully over (it ended in 1954). But fifties food was probably still on the menu when you were small. Tins of everything, stacked high. For flavour, take your pick: ketchup, brown sauce, or salad cream. Olive oil? It's still in the bathroom cabinet. Still, some dishes were worth keeping: who can resist a coronation chicken sandwich?

### Milkshakes
Thick, creamy and an ideal hiding place for a lethal dose of poison. That's what the CIA thought when they plotted to slip a pill into Castro's beloved chocolate milkshake. Fortunately for the Cuban leader, the pill stuck to the freezer door.

Chop Suey

Real cream cakes

### Bananas
In the 1950s, Gros Michel bananas – the dominant banana sold – were wiped out by the Panama disease, nearly destroying the banana industry.

Peaches

### Frosties
Introduced in 1954 as Sugar Frosted Flakes, this new cereal was an instant hit – as was Tony the Tiger.

Frozen chicken

### Tinned pineapple
Think pineapple, think Hawaii. Pineapples are still cultivated there, although the state's last cannery closed in 2006.

### Spam fritters
Dubbed the 'Miracle Meat' when it was introduced in the late thirties, Spam is no longer made in the UK but it's still popular. Worldwide, around 7 billion cans have been sold; 44,000 cans are still produced every hour.

Baked Alaska

Devilled eggs

Coronation chicken

### Hamburgers
In the US during WWII, hamburgers were briefly rebranded 'liberty steaks' in a renewed bout of food-as-propaganda. In World War I, sauerkraut was 'liberty cabbage' while French fries became 'freedom fries' during the Iraq war.

# Pre-war Chocolate

Many of the chocolate bars we enjoy today were dreamed up long before WWII – though recipes, sizes and names have mostly been given a tweak or two over the decades to keep them as our newsagent favourites.

| | |
|---|---|
| 1800s | **Fry's Chocolate Cream**<br>The first chocolate bars to be mass-produced. |
| 1905 | Cadbury Dairy Milk |
| 1908 | Bourneville |
| 1914 | Fry's Turkish Delight |
| 1920 | Flake |
| 1926 | Cadbury's Fruit & Nut |
| 1927 | **Jaffa Cake**<br>Her Majesty's Customs and Excise tried to argue that a Jaffa Cake is a biscuit and subject to VAT. McVitie's won the day, in part because Jaffa cakes go hard when stale, unlike biscuits which go soft. |
| 1929 | Crunchie |
| 1932 | **Mars Bar**<br>Want to buy a Mars bar in the US? Ask for a Milky Way. |
| 1932 | Penguin |
| 1935 | Aero |
| 1935 | **Milky Way**<br>The Milky Way is not named after our galaxy, but instead after a type of malted milk, or milkshake as it's now known. |
| 1936 | Milky Bar |
| 1937 | **Kit Kat**<br>Before Joseph Rowntree trademarked the term 'Kit Kat' in 1911 and the snack's eventual launch in the thirties, the name was most commonly associated with a mutton pie made by pastry chef Christopher Catt. He served it in his London Kit-Cat Club during the late 17th Century. |
| 1937 | Rolo |
| 1939 | **Marathon**<br>In 1990, Marathon became Snickers: the US name since its 1930 launch (named after Frank Mars's horse). In the seventies, Mars sold a chocolate bar in the US called the Marathon – and it's still on sale here as the Curly Wurly. |

# Cars of your Childhood (Pt.1)

These are the cars that first hit the streets in the decade before you were born. Only one in five households had a car by 1960 and as cars became more reliable and popular, so the number buying second-hand grew, too. So if you travelled by car as a child, there's a strong possibility you were cooped up in one of these fifties favourites.

Austin Westminster

**Ford Prefect**
In The Hitchhiker's Guide to the Galaxy, an arriving alien picks the name Ford Prefect thinking it would be inconspicuous.

Vauxhall Velox
Sunbeam Talbot
Rover 60

**Ford Anglia**
Features on the cover of Harry Potter and the Chamber of Secrets.

Ford Consul
Hillman Minx

**Morris Minor**
Originally named Mosquito, the name was changed at the last minute as it was feared that the name would deter conservative buyers. It went on to become the first million-selling British car.

MG Magnette
Morris Oxford

**Standard Vanguard**
Named after a Navy battleship to appeal to ex-servicemen.

Austin Cambridge

**Wolseley / Riley One Point Five**
The Riley One Point Five and the Wolseley shared features including the engine, suspension and dimensions. The Riley was originally intended as a replacement for the Morris Minor.

Ford Popular

**Land Rover**
The first Land Rover was inspired by World War II jeeps, with the steering wheel in the middle. A Land Rover with tank tracks for agricultural work and a monster truck version followed.

**Austin A30**
Dubbed the steel teddy bear due to its rounded, cute appearance.

The close of the decade before you were born brought a rather less welcome motoring innovation: the parking meter. The first meters installed in 1958 in Mayfair, London (sixpence for an hour, a shilling for two), triggered the predictable result from day one: parked cars crammed onto neighbouring streets without restrictions, below.

# The Biggest Hits When You Were 10

Whistled by your father, hummed by your sister or overheard on the radio, these are the hit records as you reached double digits.

**Blockbuster** ♪ **Sweet**
Sweet borrowed the riff for this song from the Bo Diddley classic, I'm a Man.

**Cum On Feel the Noize** ♪ **Slade**
The 'noize' in question is the roar of the crowd at Slade's gigs. Although a number one in the UK, a cover of the track vastly outsold Slade's version in the US.

The Twelfth of Never ♪ Donny Osmond
Get Down ♪ Gilbert O'Sullivan
Tie a Yellow Ribbon ♪ Dawn with Tony Orlando
See My Baby Jive ♪ Wizzard
Can the Can ♪ Suzi Quatro
**Rubber Bullets** ♪ **10cc**
Rubber Bullets, much like Jailhouse Rock, is a song about an out-of-control party in a county prison.

Skweeze Me Pleeze Me ♪ Slade
Welcome Home ♪ Peters and Lee
Young Love ♪ Donny Osmond
Daydreamer ♪ David Cassidy
**Merry Xmas Everybody** ♪ **Slade**
Slade recorded Merry Xmas Everybody in the middle of a hot New York summer after drummer Don Powell lost his memory in a car crash and wanted to get playing again as soon as possible.

# Tech Breakthroughs Before You Turned 25

Much of the technology we use today stands on the shoulders of the inventions made while you were small. Here are some of the most notable advances.

| | |
|---|---|
| 1964 | Plasma display |
| 1965 | Hypertext (http) |
| 1966 | Computer RAM |
| 1967 | **Hand-held calculator**<br>Hand-held, maybe: pocket-sized, definitely not. That came along in 1972 thanks to Clive Sinclair and his slimline Executive model – just one invention in his phenomenally productive career. |
| 1967 | **Computer mouse**<br>Doug Engelbart patented an early version of his 'X-Y indicator' in 1967. By the time a (very large) mouse became available with a Xerox computer in 1981, the patent had expired. |
| 1969 | Laser printer |
| 1971 | Email |
| 1973 | Mobile phone |
| 1976 | Apple Computer |
| 1979 | Barcodes |
| 1979 | Compact disc |
| 1982 | **Emoticons**<br>The inventor of the smiley emoticon hands out 'Smiley' cookies every Sept 19th – the anniversary of its first use. |
| 1983 | Internet |
| 1983 | Microsoft Word |
| 1984 | LCD projector |
| 1984 | Apple Macintosh |
| 1985 | **Sinclair C5**<br>Despite a body and a chassis designed by Lotus and assembled by Hoover, the ahead-of-its-time Sinclair C5 was plagued with problems including poor battery life, the inability to climb gentle hills and safety concerns. |

# On the Silver Screen When You Were 11

From family favourites to the films you weren't allowed to watch, these are the movies that drew the praise and crowds when you turned 11.

Butley  Alan Bates, Jessica Tandy
The Marseille Contract  Michael Caine, Anthony Quinn
Swallows and Amazons  Virginia McKenna, Ronald Fraser
Juggernaut  Richard Harris, Omar Sharif
**The Man with the Golden Gun**  Roger Moore, Christopher Lee
**The film was so poorly-received it almost ended the spy franchise.**

Callan  Edward Woodward, Eric Porter
Earthquake  Charlton Heston, Ava Gardner
Brief Encounter  Richard Burton, Sophia Loren
The Parallax View  Warren Beatty, Hume Cronyn
The Conversation  Gene Hackman, John Cazale
Chinatown  Jack Nicholson, Faye Dunaway
The Four Musketeers  Michael York, Raquel Welch
The Towering Inferno  Paul Newman, Steve McQueen
The Great Gatsby  Robert Redford, Mia Farrow
Zardoz  Sean Connery, Charlotte Rampling
**Young Frankenstein**  Gene Wilder, Madeline Kahn
Marty Feldman improvised the 'moving hump' gag without telling the crew. It was weeks before they caught on to what he was doing. They found the joke so funny they kept it in the film.

Death Wish  Charles Bronson, Hope Lange
Stardust  David Essex, Adam Faith
The Odessa File  Jon Voight, Maximilian Schell
**Blazing Saddles**  Cleavon Little, Gene Wilder
Wilder only agreed to act in Blazing Saddles if Mel Brooks considered his idea for another movie – Young Frankenstein.

**The Godfather Part II**  Al Pacino, Robert De Niro
Robert De Niro and Marlon Brando both won Oscars for playing Vito Corleone – a double-act only repeated by Heath Ledger and Joaquin Phoenix who both excelled as The Joker.

Great Expectations  Michael York, Sarah Miles

# Comics When You Were Small

Did you spend your childhood hopping from one foot to the other, longing for the next edition of your favourite comic to appear on the shelves? If so, these may be the titles you were waiting for.

**Knockout** ✹ (1939-1963, 1971-73)
Knockout Comics (or Knock-Out as they were originally known) ran for 24 years before merging into Valiant. However, you may remember it from its 1971 revival (without the hyphen!). Unlike most comics of the early 70s, every page was in colour.

Twinkle ✹ (1968-1999)
The Eagle ✹ (1950-1969)
**Robin** ✹ (1953-1969)
Some of the most popular Robin comic strips included BBC children's characters Andy Pandy and the Flower Pot Men.

The Hornet ✹ (1963-1976)
**Look And Learn** ✹ (1962-1982)
The first issue of Look and Learn featured a photograph of a very young Prince Charles on the front cover.

TV Comic ✹ (1951-1984)
Jack and Jill ✹ (1954-1985)
Tiger ✹ (1954-1985)
The Topper ✹ (1953-1990)
Whizzer And Chips ✹ (1969-1990)
Jackie ✹ (1964-1993)
**The Beezer** ✹ (1956-1993)
For the first 25 years of its run, Beezer – companion to Topper – was printed in large-format A3.

Buster ✹ (1960-2000)
Bunty ✹ (1958-2001)
The Dandy ✹ (1937-2012)
**Beano** ✹ (1938-present)
The most valuable copies of the first issue of Beano fetch over £17,000 at auction. There are only 20 left in the world today.

# Around the UK

Double digits at last: you're old enough to eavesdrop on adults and scan the headlines. These may be some of the earliest national news stories you remember.

✦ Hijacked helicopter airlifts three IRA prisoners to freedom
✦ Bloody Sunday inquest absolves British army of civilian shootings
✦ 1.6 million workers join one-day strike over wage freeze
✦ Queen Elizabeth opens new London Bridge
✦ New power-sharing system for Northern Ireland agreed
✦ Princess Anne weds Captain Mark Phillips at Westminster Abbey
✦ People of Northern Ireland vote to remain part of UK
✦ Goods and services tax VAT introduced as UK joins EEC
✦ Northern Ireland abolishes capital punishment
✦ Packed express train derails at Ealing – 10 dead, 94 injured
✦ British Library founded
✦ UK's first commercial radio station LBC goes on air
✦ Temporary agreement on British catch quota ends second Cod War
✦ Dalai Lama makes first visit to UK
✦ Thalidomide victims get £20m payout after long court case
✦ IRA's letter- and car-bomb campaign rocks London
✦ Britain officially joins the EEC
✦ Pink Floyd releases best-selling album The Dark Side of the Moon
✦ First women stockbrokers admitted to Stock Exchange
✦ First Open University degree awarded
✦ British Governor of Bermuda and assistant murdered

*Born this year:*
❧ Northern comedian Peter Kay born near Bolton
❧ World champion distance runner Paula Radcliffe born in Cheshire

# UK Buildings

Some were loathed then, loved now; others, the reverse. Some broke new architectural ground, others helped to power a nation or entertain. All of them were built before you were 40.

| | |
|---|---|
| 1963 | Bankside Power Station |
| 1964 | **Post Office Tower**<br>The tower was previously a designated secret under the Official Secrets Act and didn't appear on any OS maps. It was a pretty prominent secret, though, and was used as a filming location for TV and film during this time. |
| 1966 | Birmingham GPO Tower |
| 1966 | **Centre Point**<br>One of London's first skyscrapers, 24-storey Centre Point was a lightning rod for those protesting the plight of the homeless. Built speculatively, it stood empty until the mid seventies, awaiting a tenant with deep pockets. The homeless charity Centrepoint uses its emblematic name. |
| 1966 | **Severn Bridge**<br>Grade I listed, and since 2018, free to cross (both ways!). |
| 1967 | Queen Elizabeth Hall |
| 1974 | **Birmingham Library**<br>Looked like 'a place where books are incinerated, not kept' said Prince Charles. It was demolished in 2013. |
| 1976 | National Exhibition Centre (NEC) |
| 1976 | **Brent Cross Centre**<br>The UK's first American-style indoor shopping centre. The car park was used for the James Bond film Tomorrow Never Dies. |
| 1980 | NatWest Tower |
| 1982 | Barbican Centre |
| 1986 | Lloyd's Building |
| 1991 | **One Canada Square, London**<br>This Canary Wharf icon spent 20 years as the UK's tallest building before The Shard stole its thunder. |
| 2004 | **30 St Mary Axe (The Gherkin), London**<br>During construction, the remains of a Roman teenage girl were found buried on the site. |
| 2012 | The Shard, London |

# Early Radio 1 DJs

Do you remember the first time you heard 'the exciting new sound of Radio 1'? Replacing the BBC Light Programme in 1967, it soon won over the UK's youth to become the world's most popular station, and the DJs – all men until Annie Nightingale joined in 1970 – became household names.

### Tony Blackburn
The man who started it all with those immortal words and span the first disc (Flowers in the Rain, by The Move). And don't forget his canine co-presenter, Arnold.

### John Peel
Peel's life-long service to music is well known. But before this took off, his aspiration to be a journalist while selling insurance in Texas led him to bluff his way into the midnight news conference where Lee Harvey Oswald was paraded before the press.

Keith Skues
### Ed Stewart
For children of the seventies, Ed Stewart means Crackerjack; but for those of us born earlier, it was Junior Choice on Saturday mornings where we'd get to know 'Stewpot'.

Mike Raven
Jimmy Young
Dave Cash
### Kenny Everett
Everett was a Radio 1 DJ for less than three years before being sacked. He also appeared in 1980 on Just a Minute and was given the subject of marbles. Nicholas Parsons let him talk (while hesitating, repeating *and* deviating) for 90 seconds as a joke – assisted by the other panellists. He wasn't on the show again.

Terry Wogan
Duncan Johnson
Tommy Vance
### Emperor Rosko
'Your groovy host from the West coast, here to clear up your skin and mess up your mind. It'll make you feel good all over!' – Rosko, aka Mike Pasternak, introducing his Midday Spin show.

Pete Murray
Bob Holness

# Female Wimbledon Winners

Aged 15 in 1887, Lottie Dod was the youngest to win Wimbledon. Aged 37 in 1908, Charlotte Cooper Sterry was the oldest. These are the winners when you too were still in with a (slim) chance! Men, PTO!

| | |
|---|---|
| 1978-79 | Martina Navratilova |
| 1980 | Evonne Goolagong Cawley |
| 1981 | **Chris Evert Lloyd**<br>Nicknamed the Ice Maiden, Evert was the first tennis player to win 1,000 matches and the first female tennis player to reach $1million in career prize money. |
| 1982-87 | Martina Navratilova |
| 1988-89 | Steffi Graf |
| 1990 | Martina Navratilova |
| 1991-93 | Steffi Graf |
| 1994 | Conchita Martínez |
| 1995-96 | Steffi Graf |
| 1997 | **Martina Hingis**<br>Hingis' mother had tennis dreams for her daughter before she was born; she named her after Martina Navratilova. Hingis was playing tennis by age two and at 12 years old, she became the youngest player to win a major junior title. |
| 1998 | **Jana Novotná**<br>Aside from her 1998 victory, Novotná is fondly remembered for being comforted by the Duchess of Kent after her Wimbledon finals loss to Steffi Graf in 1993. Novotná died from cancer in 2017 at the age of just 49. |
| 1999 | Lindsay Davenport |
| 2000-01 | Venus Williams |

# Wimbledon: The Men

In the men's tournament, Becker won at the tender age of 17. At the top end, Federer won in 2017 at the age of 35. But in 1909, in the amateur era, Arthur Gore was a nimble 41 years young – giving us our 'winning window' of 17 to 41.

| | |
|---|---|
| 1976-80 | **Björn Borg**<br>Sweden's Ice Man dominated the late seventies with his unusual baseline play, incredible fitness and good looks. Retirement at the age of 26 didn't suit him and at 34 he attempted a no-practice comeback with the same wooden racket (everyone else by then was using graphite). Unsurprisingly, it didn't pan out – unlike his revitalised and highly successful fashion label. |
| 1981 | John McEnroe |
| 1982 | Jimmy Connors |
| 1983-84 | John McEnroe |
| 1985-86 | **Boris Becker** |
| 1987 | Pat Cash |
| 1988 | Stefan Edberg |
| 1989 | Boris Becker |
| 1990 | Stefan Edberg |
| 1991 | Michael Stich |
| 1992 | **Andre Agassi**<br>Agassi started losing his hair at 19 and wore hairpieces to hide it. The night before the 1990 French Open final, his wig was damaged. He wore it during the match but was so worried about it falling off that he lost. |
| 1993-95 | Pete Sampras |
| 1996 | Richard Krajicek |
| 1997-'00 | Pete Sampras |
| 2001 | **Goran Ivanišević**<br>Ivanišević – unlucky? He once stood on a seashell; his foot became infected and needed surgery. Another time, when retrieving his forgotten tennis racket, the door unexpectedly shut and broke several of his fingers. |
| 2002 | Lleyton Hewitt |
| 2003-07 | Roger Federer |

# Books of the Decade

Ten years that took you from kids' adventure books to dense works of profundity – or maybe just grown-up adventures! How many did you read when they were first published?

| | |
|---|---|
| 1973 | Gravity's Rainbow by Thomas Pynchon |
| 1973 | Crash: A Novel by J G Ballard |
| 1974 | **Tinker, Tailor, Soldier, Spy by John le Carré**<br>David Cornwell, the man behind the pseudonym John le Carré, drew on his personal experience working for MI5 and MI6. He appeared as an extra in the film of the book. |
| 1974 | **Carrie by Stephen King**<br>Carrie was King's first novel, published when he was 26. He disliked the first draft and threw it in the bin; his wife found it and encouraged him to continue with the story. |
| 1974 | The Bottle Factory Outing by Beryl Bainbridge |
| 1975 | Shogun by James Clavell |
| 1975 | The Periodic Table by Primo Levi |
| 1976 | Interview with the Vampire by Anne Rice |
| 1977 | Song of Solomon by Toni Morrison |
| 1977 | The Shining by Stephen King |
| 1978 | The World According to Garp by John Irving |
| 1978 | The Sea, The Sea by Iris Murdoch |
| 1978 | Tales of the City by Armistead Maupin |
| 1979 | **The Hitchhiker's Guide to the Galaxy by Douglas Adams**<br>If 42 is the meaning of life, what's the meaning of 42? Nothing. Adams said it was simply a random number he chose. There's a message in there somewhere... |
| 1979 | A Bend in the River by V S Naipaul |
| 1979 | Sophie's Choice by William Styron |
| 1980 | A Confederacy of Dunces by John Kennedy Toole |
| 1980 | The Name of the Rose by Umberto Eco |
| 1981 | Midnight's Children by Salman Rushdie |
| 1982 | The Color Purple by Alice Walker |
| 1982 | **Schindler's Ark by Thomas Keneally**<br>Keneally wrote Schindler's Ark – later retitled Schindler's List – after he met Holocaust survivor Leopold Page. Schindler is credited with saving over 1,000 lives. |

# Around the UK

Here's a round-up of the most newsworthy events from across the country in the year you turned (sweet) 16.

- Sex Pistols Sid Vicious dies of drug overdose
- Lord Mountbatten killed by IRA bomb
- Margaret Thatcher becomes UK's first female prime minister
- IRA blast at Warrenpoint near Newry kills 18 British soldiers
- UK's first public naturist beach opens in Brighton
- The Times publishes again after year-long dispute
- Elton John first western rock star to perform in USSR
- UK controls on buying and using foreign currency lifted
- Lorry drivers' strike causes food and fuel shortages
- Shadow Northern Ireland Secretary Airey Neave killed by car bomb (right)
- Anti-racism protester Blair Peach killed by police
- St Lucia gains independence from UK
- Athlete Sebastian Coe sets new record for mile
- First man-powered plane crosses English Channel
- Anthony Blunt 'fourth man' in Cambridge spy ring
- Amusement park Thorpe Park opens in Surrey
- Isle of Man marks 1,000 years of Tynwald parliament
- Former Liberal leader Jeremy Thorpe cleared of attempted murder
- Government-TUC agreement ends Winter of Discontent
- London Underground's Jubilee line opens
- Scots vote for devolution; Wales says no

*Born this year:*
- Actress Rosamund Pike born in west London
- Rugby union star Jonny Wilkinson born in Frimley, Surrey
- Jazz musician Jamie Cullum born in Rochford, Essex

Airey Neave, a WWII war hero who became Shadow Secretary of State for Northern Ireland, was murdered by the Irish National Liberation Army on 30 March 1979. A magnetic car bomb killed Neave as he left the Palace of Westminster. Margaret Thatcher, who's campaign to become leader was managed by Neave, called him 'staunch, brave, true, strong.' She is accompanied above at Neave's funeral service by Ian Gow, Thatcher's private secretary and colleague of Neave. Gow was assassinated in 1990

# Stamps When You Were Young

Stamp collecting was the first serious hobby for many 20th century children. Commemorative issues weren't issued until the twenties, but soon became highly collectible – and the perfect gift for uncles in need of inspiration. These stamps may well have started your collection.

| | |
|---|---|
| 1924-5 | **British Empire Exhibition**<br>Designed to showcase Britain's strengths in an era of declining global influence, the exhibition left a legacy: the Empire Stadium (later renamed Wembley Stadium). The stamps were the UK's first commemorative issue, sixty years after the USA did the same. |
| 1929 | **9th Universal Postal Union Congress, London**<br>Arguably of little interest to few outside philatelic circles, this was the first of several self-referential issues over successive decades. See also the Inter-Parliamentary stamps first issued in 1957. |
| 1935 | George V Silver Jubilee |
| 1937 | George VI Coronation |
| 1940 | **Centenary of the first adhesive postage stamp**<br>Everyone has heard of the first adhesive stamp, issued in 1840: the Penny Black. (Perforations didn't come along until the 1854 Penny Red.) The glue on commemorative stamps contained around 14 calories! |
| 1946 | Victory |
| 1948 | Royal Silver Wedding |
| 1948 | Olympic Games |
| 1949 | The 75th Anniversary of the Universal Postal Union |
| 1951 | Festival of Britain |
| 1951 | George VI (high value 'definitives') |
| 1953 | The coronation of Queen Elizabeth II |
| 1955 | Castles (high value 'definitives') |
| 1957 | **World Scout Jamboree**<br>Held in Sutton Coldfield; 50,000 Scouts attended. After heavy rain, the US Air Force was called in to help. |
| 1957 | 46th Inter-Parliamentary Union Conference |
| 1958 | 6th British Empire and Commonwealth Games |

# The Biggest Hits When You Were 16

The songs that topped the charts when you turned 16 might not be in your top 10 these days, but you'll probably remember them!

### YMCA ♪ Village People
The Village People were livid at Donald Trump's use of their hit song at his rallies, labelling it as abusive.

### Heart of Glass ♪ Blondie
### Tragedy ♪ Bee Gees
### I Will Survive ♪ Gloria Gaynor
I Will Survive was added to the national recording registry in the Library of Congress in Washington. Each year, 25 decade-old pieces of music are added to the collection based on their cultural and social impact.

### Bright Eyes ♪ Art Garfunkel
Bright Eyes was featured on the feature-length movie adaptation of Watership Down.

### Ring My Bell ♪ Anita Ward
### I Don't Like Mondays ♪ The Boomtown Rats
### We Don't Talk Anymore ♪ Cliff Richard
### Cars ♪ Gary Numan
It only took 30 minutes for Gary Numan to come up with this song, his biggest hit.

### Message in a Bottle ♪ The Police
### One Day at a Time ♪ Lena Martell
### Walking on the Moon ♪ The Police
### Another Brick in the Wall ♪ Pink Floyd

# Gameshow Hosts of the Fifties and Sixties

Many of these men were semi-permanent fixtures, their voices and catchphrases almost as familiar as our family's. Some were full-time entertainers, born to the stage; others seemed rather less suited to the spotlight!

Ted Ray... ►◄ (Joker's Wild)
and his son, Robin Ray ►◄ (Face the Music)
Peter Wheeler ►◄ (Crossword on Two, Call My Bluff)
Robert Robinson ►◄ (Brain of Britain, Ask the Family)
McDonald Hobley ►◄ (Come Dancing, It's a Knockout)
David Jacobs ►◄ (Juke Box Jury)
Shaw Taylor ►◄ (Password, Pencil and Paper)
Eamonn Andrews ►◄ (Crackerjack!)
Roy Plomley ►◄ (Many a Slip)
**Gilbert Harding ►◄ (Twenty Questions, What's My Line?)**
Harding was a teacher and policeman before working in radio and television. Resentful of his fame, Harding was once left mortified on the London Underground when he was recognised by fellow passengers who failed to notice that TS Eliot was also in the same carriage.

Bamber Gascoigne ►◄ (University Challenge)
Tommy Trinder ►◄ (Sunday Night at the Palladium)
**Bruce Forsyth ►◄ (Beat the Clock)**
Bruce Forsyth first appeared on television in 1939. He had many talents including playing the ukulele and accordion, singing, dancing and acting. In his later years, Forsyth stated that he regretted presenting so many gameshows.

Leslie Crowther ►◄ (Billy Cotton Band Show, Crackerjack)
**Bob Monkhouse ►◄ (The Golden Shot)**
While serving in the RAF, Bob Monkhouse drafted a letter to the BBC from his group captain, stating that 18-year-old Monkhouse was a war hero and deserved an audition. His group captain signed the letter without reading it; Monkhouse got his audition.

Hughie Green ►◄ (Opportunity Knocks)
Derek Batey ►◄ (Mr and Mrs)
Wilfred Pickles ►◄ (radio show Have a Go)

# Kitchen Inventions

The 20th-century kitchen was a playground for food scientists and engineers with new labour-saving devices and culinary shortcuts launched every year. Here are some your parents – and now you – wouldn't be without.

| | |
|---|---|
| 1929 | **Dishwasher**<br>The first hand-operated dishwasher was created in 1885 by inventor and socialite, Josephine Cochrane, who was tired of her servants chipping her fine china. In 1929, Miele brought out an electric, top-loading model. Front-loading and drying functions followed in 1940; automation in 1960. |
| 1937 | Blender |
| 1939 | Pressure cooker |
| 1940 | Chest freezer |
| 1945 | **Fridge**<br>If you think today's American-style fridges are big, consider the Large Hadron Collider in Geneva. With a circumference of 17 miles and 9,300 magnets, it's chilled to -270C before use. That would definitely keep your milk cold. |
| 1948 | Kenwood mixer |
| 1955 | Automatic kettle |
| 1956 | **Non-stick pan**<br>You can thank a French angler's wife for your non-stick pans: it was she who noticed her husband's habit of coating his gear in non-stick Teflon, and suggested he did the same to her pans. Scrambled egg fans owe her a life-long debt. |
| 1960 | **Tupperware**<br>In 1960, Tupperware parties arrived in the UK. Earl Tupper's 1948 invention took off when a US single mother called Brownie Wise started home sales and the social selling concept proved equally successful here. This icon of female entrepreneurship was dismissed in 1958 for being too outspoken. |
| 1974 | Microwave |
| 1974 | Food processor |
| 1976 | **Deep fat fryer**<br>The Egyptians, Romans and Greeks were all known to have been keen on deep frying their food – often items that look uncommonly like today's doughnuts (minus the jam). |

# Around the World When You Turned 18

These are the headlines from around the globe as you were catapulted into adulthood.

- 52 US hostages released after 444 days of Tehran Embassy siege
- President Reagan shot and wounded in Washington DC
- US launches first reusable manned space shuttle Columbia
- France's high-speed train service TGV starts
- Egyptian President Anwar Sadat killed at Cairo military parade
- 24-hour video music channel MTV launches
- Mauritania is world's last country to abolish slavery
- Israeli warplanes bomb PLO targets in Beirut and south Lebanon
- Simon & Garfunkel reunite for Central Park concert in New York
- Crowded passenger train derails in Bihar, India, killing over 500
- Mexico City Zoo welcomes first captive panda born outside China
- Socialist François Mitterrand becomes president of France
- Pope John Paul II wounded four times by gunman in Rome
- Drama in Bahamas as boxer Muhammad Ali loses last ever bout
- First recognised cases of AIDS reported in USA
- Salman Rushdie's Midnight's Children wins Booker Prize
- Action-adventure film Raiders of the Lost Ark hits cinemas

*Born this year:*
- Tennis ace Roger Federer born in Basel, Switzerland
- US singer and actor Justin Timberlake born in Memphis, Tennessee
- US singer Beyoncé Knowles born in Houston, Texas
- Duchess of Sussex born Rachel Meghan Markle in LA, California

# Toys of Your Childhood

In the sixties, the toy industry got serious: no more lead paint. New licensing models (Thunderbirds! Batman! Doctor Who!). And a Toy of the Year award – the James Bond Aston Martin car was the first winner. Hop into the seventies and you'd soon be needing some batteries to go with some of those Christmas surprises…

Sindy

Katie Kopykat

Betta Bilda

Plasticraft

**Peter Powell Stunter**

Not to be confused with the popular Radio 1 DJ, Powell was a kite designer who hit the big time after one of his models was featured on the BBC show Nationwide. His revolutionary idea was to use two lines for added control. 'It tugs at the heart strings,' he told the BBC in 2014.

Playmobil

Action Man

Duplo

**Spacehopper**

Just sneaking into this decade (if Spacehoppers can sneak): these went on sale in 1969. Sold as Hoppity Hops in the USA. In 2018, Steven Payne crossed the Alps on one. Madness.

Ping Pong

Nerf ball

Skateboards

**Lego**

The world's biggest manufacturer of tyres is not Goodyear, or Michelin – it's Lego. They produce around 300 million tiny tyres every year.

Evel Knievel Stunt Cycle

Etch-a-Sketch

Magna Doodle

Simon

**Speak and Spell**

The Speak and Spell was the first mass-produced item to include a digital signal processor, a precursor to the computers we have in our homes today.

# Around the UK

Voting. Placing a bet. Buying a legal drink. Turning 18 is serious stuff. Here's what everyone was reading about in the year you reached this milestone.

✦ Over 100 small tornadoes hit north Wales and England
✦ Rebel Labour and Liberal MPs set up Social Democratic Party
✦ Yorkshire Ripper Peter Sutcliffe found guilty of killing 13 women
✦ UK's Bucks Fizz wins Eurovision with 'Making Your Mind Up'
✦ Maze prison hunger strikes end, leaving 10 dead
✦ The Times bought by Aussie newspaper mogul Rupert Murdoch
✦ Steve Davis wins World Snooker Championship for the first time
✦ Racial inequality sparks Brixton riots – 300 hurt, £7.5m damage
✦ Futuristic sports car DeLorean assembled in Northern Ireland
✦ Fire at Goodge Street tube station – one dead, 16 injured
✦ Homebase opens its first DIY store in Croydon
✦ Penlee lifeboat and Union Starcrew drown in storm off Cornwall
✦ Over 7,000 runners take part in first London Marathon
✦ Teenager fires blanks at Queen as she rides to Troop the Colour
✦ Prince Charles weds Lady Diana Spencer at St Paul's Cathedral
✦ BBC sitcom Only Fools and Horses first seen on our screens
✦ British Leyland Longbridge dispute ends with 7,000 laid off
✦ First death from AIDS recorded in UK
✦ UB40 release single 'One in Ten' about UK unemployment rate
✦ Oscar-winner Chariots of Fire released in UK cinemas
✦ 250,000 protest against US nuclear bases in UK at CND rally

*Born this year:*
🎂 Super-tall England striker Peter Crouch born in Macclesfield
🎂 Golden Globe-winning actor Tom Hiddleston born in London
🎂 Princess Anne's daughter equestrian Zara Phillips born in London

Prince Charles had only met Diana Frances Spencer around a dozen times before he proposed to the 19-year-old earl's daughter in 1981, followed by the wedding in July of that year. A whirlwind, certainly, but romance? The pressure to find a bride of the right standing was mounting after a decade in which he had dated women whatever their eligibility (including Diana's elder sister, and Camilla Parker Bowles). And so, despite his doubts, he

# Medical Advances Before You Were 21

A girl born in the UK in 1921 had a life expectancy of 59.6 years (boys: 55.6). By 2011 that was up to 82.8 (79 for boys), thanks to medical advances including many of these.

| | |
|---|---|
| 1963 | **Valium**<br>Valium was famously dubbed 'mother's little helper' by The Rolling Stones. Valium was hailed as a wonder drug as it worked was a far less risky alternative to barbiturates. |
| 1963 | Lung transplant, artificial heart |
| 1964 | Measles vaccine |
| 1965 | **Portable defibrillator**<br>CPR on TV is successful one time in two, a 2009 study found: roughly the same as reality. However, the lack of follow-up or age-related differences on TV means people's expectation for a life-saving result is unrealistically high. |
| 1966 | Pancreas transplant |
| 1967 | Heart transplant |
| 1968 | Liver transplant, Controlled drug delivery |
| 1969 | **Cochlear implant**<br>Cochlear implants aren't always a success. Some can't get on with them; others believe they undermine deaf culture. |
| 1969 | Balloon catheter |
| 1971 | CAT scan |
| 1972 | Insulin pump |
| 1973 | MRI scanning, Laser eye surgery (LASIK) |
| 1974 | Depo-Provera contraceptive injection |
| 1974 | **Liposuction**<br>Liposuction did not take off until 1985 when techniques had improved to decrease the chance of serious bleeding. |
| 1976 | First commercial PET scanner |
| 1978 | Test-tube baby (IVF) |
| 1980 | MRI whole body scanner |
| 1981 | Heart-lung transplant |
| 1982 | Artificial heart |
| 1983 | DNA fingerprinting |

# Popular Girls' Names

**20** If you started a family at a young age, these are the names you're most likely to have chosen. And even if you didn't pick them, a lot of British parents did!

Sarah
Claire
Nicola
Emma
Lisa
Joanne
Michelle
Helen
**Samantha**
At number 9, Samantha's first appearance is among the highest of the century. She'll stay around until 2003.
Karen
Amanda
Rachel
Louise
Julie
Clare
Rebecca
Sharon
Victoria
Caroline
Susan
Alison
Catherine
Elizabeth
Deborah
Donna
Tracey
Tracy
**Rising and falling stars:**
Just like the boys, several names are all-too-briefly on the lips of many new parents: Vanessa, Nichola, Tara, Clair and Sonia.

# Animals Extinct in Your Lifetime

Billions of passenger pigeons once flew the US skies. By 1914, they had been trapped to extinction. Not every species dies at our hands, but it's a sobering roll-call. (Date is year last known alive or declared extinct).

| | |
|---|---|
| 1963 | Kākāwahie honeycreeper, Hawaii |
| 1964 | South Island snipe, New Zealand |
| 1966 | Arabian ostrich |
| 1967 | Saint Helena earwig |
| 1967 | **Yellow blossom pearly mussel, USA** <br> Habitat loss and pollution proved terminal for this resident of Tennessee. |
| 1968 | Mariana fruit bat (Guam) |
| 1971 | Lake Pedder earthworm, Tasmania |
| 1972 | Bushwren, New Zealand |
| 1977 | Siamese flat-barbelled catfish, Thailand |
| 1979 | Yunnan Lake newt, China |
| 1981 | Southern gastric-brooding frog, Australia |
| 1986 | Las Vegas dace |
| 1989 | Golden toad (see right) |
| 1990 | Atitlán grebe, Guatemala |
| 1990 | Dusky seaside sparrow, East Coast USA |
| 1990s | Rotund rocksnail, USA |
| 2000 | **Pyrenean ibex, Iberia** <br> For a few minutes in 2003 this species was brought back to life through cloning, but sadly the newborn female ibex died. |
| 2001 | Caspian tiger, Central Asia |
| 2008 | Saudi gazelle |
| 2012 | **Pinta giant tortoise** <br> The rarest creature in the world for the latter half of his 100-year life, Lonesome George lived out his days in the Galapagos as the last remaining Pinta tortoise. |
| 2016 | Bramble Cay melomys (a Great Barrier Reef rodent) |

The observed history of the golden toad is brief and tragic. It wasn't discovered until 1964, abundant in a pristine area of Costa Rica. By 1989 it had gone, a victim of rising temperatures.

# Popular Boys' Names

Here are the top boys' names for this year. In many instances it's merely a reshuffle of the popular names from the previous decade; but in the lower reaches, change is afoot...

**Paul**
After John, then David, came Paul: the nation's favourite name, but he'd keep the spot for less than a decade.

Mark
David
Andrew
Richard
Christopher
James
Simon
Michael
Matthew
Stephen
Lee
John
Robert
Darren
Daniel
Steven
Jason
Nicholas
Jonathan
Ian
Neil
Peter
Stuart
Anthony
Martin
Kevin

**Rising and falling stars:**
It's rare that names become popular enough to make the Top 100 only to fall out of favour as quickly as they came. Rarer still to have three flashes-in-the-pan: Glen, Brett and Damian.

# Popular Movies When You Were 21

The biggest stars in the biggest movies: these are the films the nation was enjoying as you entered adulthood.

Gremlins 🎞️ Zach Galligan, Phoebe Cates
Beverly Hills Cop 🎞️ Eddie Murphy, Judge Reinhold
Romancing the Stone 🎞️ Kathleen Turner, Michael Douglas
Footloose 🎞️ Kevin Bacon, Lori Singer
Another Country 🎞️ Rupert Everett, Colin Firth
**Ghostbusters** 🎞️ Bill Murray, Dan Aykroyd
Nearly every word from Murray is an ad-lib. In fact, most of the actors were given the nod to improvise as much as possible.

Amadeus 🎞️ Tom Hulce, F Murray Abraham
The Company of Wolves 🎞️ Sarah Patterson, Angela Lansbury
**Purple Rain** 🎞️ Prince, Apollonia
Prince made co-star Apollonia promise to break up with David Lee Roth and not date anybody famous during the promotion of Purple Rain. He also dictated what she wore and when she could eat.

A Passage to India 🎞️ Judy Davis, Victor Bannerjee
Splash 🎞️ Tom Hanks, Darryl Hannah
Paris, Texas 🎞️ Harry Dean Stanton, Dean Stockwell
Police Academy 🎞️ Steve Guttenberg, GW Bailey
Against All Odds 🎞️ Rachel Ward, Jeff Bridges
The Killing Fields 🎞️ Haing S Ngor, John Malkovich
**The Karate Kid** 🎞️ Ralph Macchio, William Zabka
Macchio was given the famous 'wax on, wax off' car as a present and brought it out of retirement for the Cobra Kai TV series.

The Bounty 🎞️ Anthony Hopkins, Mel Gibson
A Private Function 🎞️ Maggie Smith, Michael Palin
The Natural 🎞️ Robert Redford, Glenn Close
This Is Spinal Tap 🎞️ Michael McKean, Christopher Guest
**The Terminator** 🎞️ Arnold Schwarzenegger, Linda Hamilton
Linda Hamilton broke her ankle before shooting The Terminator. She spent most of the shoot in pain and had to film all her action scenes at the end of the production schedule.

The Never Ending Story 🎞️ Noah Hathaway, Barret Oliver

# Around the UK

A selection of national headlines from the year you turned 21. But how many can you remember?

- British Telecom privatised – 50% shares sold to investors
- Miners walk out in long battle over pit closure threat
- Financial Times Stock Exchange FTSE 100 Index set up
- First Virgin Atlantic plane takes off
- Half pence coin withdrawn from circulation
- Church of England supports ordaining women as priests
- Skaters Torvill and Dean win Olympic gold with Boléro routine
- Police and miners clash at Orgreave colliery – 64 injured (right)
- Band Aid charity single Do They Know It's Christmas? released
- Brunei becomes independent of UK
- York Minster roof set ablaze by lightning bolt
- Magnitude 5.4 earthquake shakes north Wales
- South African runner Zola Budd granted British citizenship
- IRA Brighton hotel bomb targets Tory cabinet, killing five
- Sinn Fein president Gerry Adams wounded in loyalist shooting
- One dead, 11 injured in 294-day London Libyan Embassy siege
- Princess Diana gives birth to second son Harry, Duke of Sussex
- UK geneticist Alec Jeffreys discovers DNA fingerprinting
- Police drama The Bill airs on ITV
- Government bans union membership at Cheltenham GCHQ
- Civil servant Sarah Tisdall jailed for cruise missile leak

*Born this year:*
- TV personality and daughter of Ozzy, Kelly Osbourne born in London
- Singer and TV presenter Olly Murs born in Witham, Essex
- The Crown actress Claire Foy born in Stockport

For years after the events of 18 June 1984, the establishment narrative largely held: thousands of violent picketers at Orgreave Colliery had confronted the police in their attempt to stop deliveries of coal. Truncheon and horse charges and the use of snatch squads were made in self-defence as the rioters ran amok.

As the decades passed, the truth emerged. Trials collapsed and compensation was paid as police evidence proved unreliable and malpractice uncovered; evidence was prefabricated and links at a senior level between the manner of policing at both Orgreave and Hillsborough were revealed.

# The Biggest Hits When You Were 21

The artists you love at 21 are with you for life. How many of these hits from this milestone year can you still hum or sing in the bath?

Pipes of Peace ♪ Paul McCartney

Relax ♪ Frankie Goes to Hollywood

99 Red Balloons ♪ Nena

**Hello ♪ Lionel Richie**

Lionel Richie was instructed to write this song after Ritchie jokily crooned the eponymous line at his producer.

The Reflex ♪ Duran Duran

**Wake Me Up Before You Go-Go ♪ Wham!**

Andrew Ridgeley accidentally came up with title for this song when he accidentally left his mother a note saying 'wake me up up...' Ridgeley took the idea to complete the song's title.

Two Tribes ♪ Frankie Goes to Hollywood

Careless Whisper ♪ George Michael

Freedom ♪ Wham!

**I Feel for You ♪ Chaka Khan**

In order to meet Chaka Khan, I Feel for You songwriter Prince rang her on the phone and pretended to be her good friend Sylvester Stallone.

I Should Have Known Better ♪ Jim Diamond

**The Power of Love ♪ Frankie Goes to Hollywood**

The Power of Love marked a stellar year for Frankie Goes to Hollywood when it became their third number one of 1984.

Do They Know It's Christmas ♪ Band Aid

# Popular Food in the 1960s

Convenient ready meals, 'fancy foreign food'... the sixties menu had it all. The chemists joined the dinner party, too, with additives and processes that made our new favourites easy and cheap to produce. We'd take a while to work out if this was always such a good idea!

Vesta curry or Chow Mein

**Lager**
'Lager' comes from the German word 'lagern', meaning 'to store', as lager takes longer to produce than other ales.

Coco Pops

**Fish fingers**
The largest fish finger ever made was 6ft long and weighed 136 kg. No word on whether the chef dipped it in ketchup.

**Spaghetti Bolognese**
You shouldn't include oregano, basil or garlic in the 'ragu' (not bolognese). And for goodness' sake, use tagliatelle, not spaghetti. Or... accept that it is as inauthentic as the Vesta curry and enjoy, like millions of Brits learned to do in the sixties.

Chicken Tikka Masala

**Cheese and onion crisps**
The first flavoured crisps were created by Joe 'Spud' Murphy (founder of Irish brand Taytos) in the late 1950s.

Crêpe Suzette

Chicken liver pâté

**Angel Delight**
Angel Delight doubled the dessert market when it was invented in 1967. Wallace and Gromit gave it another push in 1999.

Fray Bentos pies

Instant coffee

**Frozen vegetables**
Clarence Birdseye was the first person to freeze food for mass production, having got the idea from an Inuit in 1912.

Swedish meatballs

**White bread**
A new Chorleywood process introduced enzymes and additives and high-speed mixing. The result? Soft, cheap bread that sticks to the roof of your mouth. A nation couldn't get enough of it.

# Fashion in the Sixties

As a child, you (generally) wear what you're given. It's only in hindsight, on fading slides, that you recognize that your outfits carried the fashion imprint of the day. Whether you were old or bold enough to carry off a pair of bell bottoms, though, is a secret that between you and your photo albums!

Shift dresses
### Mini skirt
Popularised by Mary Quant who named the skirt after her favourite car – although not everyone was a fan. Coco Chanel described the skirt as 'just awful', and it was banned in some European countries.

Five-point cut
### Vidal Sassoon
Sassoon had a temper. He would give clients a slap of a comb if they touched their hair while he was cutting it.

John Bates
### Biba
Biba started as a mail order business, advertising a pink gingham dress in the Daily Mirror. 17,000 orders were placed and a shop was opened. On its opening day, the store sold out of its only product line.

St Michael American Tan tights
Dr Scholl
Orlon, Crimplene, Terylene, Spandex, PVC and Vinyl
Paper dresses
Twiggy
### Jackie Kennedy
In 1962, Jackie Kennedy wore a leopard print coat which caused a spike in demand for leopard skin, leading to the death of up to 250,000 leopards. The coat's designer, Oleg Cassini, felt guilty about it for the rest of his life.

### Little black dress
First introduced by Coco Chanel in the 1920s, the little black dress received a fifties update from Christian Dior. Audrey Hepburn's LBD sold for £467,200 in 2006.

Jean Shrimpton
Jane Birkin

# Around the World When You Turned 25

By your mid-twenties, TV coverage of news in far-flung places brought global stories into our homes almost as fast as they happened. How many do you remember?

+ Australia celebrates bicentenary of its founding
+ Israeli commandos kill PLO deputy leader Abu Jihad in Tunisia
+ First World AIDS Day held to raise awareness of HIV
+ Francois Mitterand re-elected as President of France
+ Soviet troops start to withdraw from Afghanistan
+ Train collision at Paris Gare de Lyon kills 56
+ Estonians hold mass singing protests against Soviet occupation
+ Osama bin Laden forms Islamist terrorist group Al-Qaeda
+ UN-brokered ceasefire ends eight-year Iran-Iraq war
+ Fires in US Yellowstone National Park scorch millions of acres
+ Canadian runner Ben Johnson fails drug test at Seoul Olympics
+ World's first Fairtrade label Max Havelaar set up in Netherlands
+ Burmese military cracks down on pro-democracy protests
+ Spitak earthquake in Armenia kills over 25,000
+ 290 die as US warship accidentally fires on Iranian airliner
+ NASA scientist advises manmade global warming has begun
+ US author Toni Morrison wins Pulitzer Prize for novel Beloved
+ Pakistan's Benazir Bhutto is first woman to head up Islamic state

*Born this year:*
& Canadian actor Michael Cera born in Brampton, Ontario
& Pop star Robyn Rihanna Fenty born in St Michael, Barbados
& German tennis player Angelique Kerber born in Bremen

# Cars of your Childhood (Pt.2)

Whether you were in one or just pointing from the side of the road, cars of the sixties truly delivered; for every trusted Hillman Imp or Vauxhall Victor, the decade boasts a glamorous Aston Martin DB5 or a covetable Jaguar E-type.

### Mini
Famously featured in the 1969 film The Italian Job, Mini manufacturer BMC didn't want the car used in the film and refused to donate any. However, the director insisted that British cars should be used in a British film and over a dozen were used.

Triumph Herald

### Vauxhall Victor
The design of the Vauxhall Victor was based on the style of American cars, which didn't appeal to everyone's taste in 1960s Britain. The car also gained a negative reputation for rusting.

Austin 1100

Sunbeam Tiger

### Aston Martin DB5
The Aston Martin DB5 has been described as the most famous car in the world, following its 1964 debut in Goldfinger. In 1968, the car used by James Bond in the film was stripped of the weapons and gadgets and resold as a used car. It was stolen in 1997 and is rumoured to be in the Middle East.

Hillman Hunter

### Lotus Elan
The Lotus Elan was designed by Ron Hickman, who subsequently left Lotus and went on to design the Black & Decker Workmate. Early versions of the Elan were also available as a kit that could be assembled by the buyer.

### Ford Cortina
The Ford Cortina was launched in 1962 and later proved to be the best-selling car of the 1970s in its Mk3 guise. Designed as a new version of the Ford Consul, the name was changed to Cortina after the Italian ski resort Cortina d'Ampezzo, host to the 1956 Winter Olympics.

Rover 3500

MGB

Vauxhall HA Viva

# Books of the Decade

Were you a voracious bookworm in your twenties? Or a more reluctant reader, only drawn by the biggest titles of the day? Here are the new titles that fought for your attention.

| | |
|---|---|
| 1983 | The Colour of Magic by Terry Pratchett |
| 1983 | Waterland by Graham Swift |
| 1984 | Money by Martin Amis |
| 1984 | Neuromancer by William Gibson |
| 1984 | The Wasp Factory by Iain Banks |
| 1985 | **The Handmaid's Tale by Margaret Atwood** |

The Communist reign of Nicolae Ceauşescu in Romania partially inspired Atwood to write The Handmaid's Tale. While he was in power, women had to have four babies; abortions were illegal, contraception was banned, and women were examined for signs of pregnancy at work.

| | |
|---|---|
| 1985 | Blood Meridian by Cormac McCarthy |
| 1985 | Perfume by Patrick Suskind |
| 1986 | The Old Devils by Kingsley Amis |
| 1986 | It by Stephen King |
| 1987 | Beloved by Toni Morrison |
| 1987 | Bonfire of the Vanities by Tom Wolfe |
| 1988 | Satanic Verses by Salman Rushdie |
| 1988 | The Alchemist by Paulo Coelho |
| 1988 | Oscar and Lucinda by Peter Carey |
| 1988 | The Swimming-Pool Library by Alan Hollinghurst |
| 1989 | A Prayer for Owen Meany by John Irving |
| 1989 | The Remains of the Day by Kazuo Ishiguro |
| 1989 | London Fields by Martin Amis |
| 1990 | Possession by AS Byatt |
| 1990 | The Buddha of Suburbia by Hanif Kureishi |
| 1991 | Regeneration by Pat Barker |
| 1991 | **American Psycho by Bret Easton Ellis** |

Ellis received death threats on account of the violent and misogynistic content. He had to indemnify his publisher from being sued by his family if he were murdered.

| | |
|---|---|
| 1992 | The Secret History by Donna Tartt |
| 1992 | All the Pretty Horses by Cormac McCarthy |

# Stamps in the Sixties

The UK hit its stride with commemorative stamps in the sixties. There were dry centenary and congress issues, but in 1965 the Postmaster General, Tony Benn, removed the need to include a large monarch portrait. The result? The kind of stamps every young collector would want.

| | |
|---|---|
| 1963 | Freedom From Hunger |
| 1963 | Lifeboat Conference |
| 1963 | Red Cross Centenary Congress |
| 1964 | Opening of the Forth Road Bridge |
| 1965 | Winston Churchill Commemoration |
| 1965 | 700th anniversary of Parliament |
| 1965 | Centenary of the Salvation Army |
| 1965 | **Antiseptic Surgery Centenary** <br> Celebrates the introduction of surgical sterilisation by Joseph Lister. |
| 1965 | Commonwealth Arts Festival |
| 1965 | 25th Anniversary of the Battle of Britain |
| 1965 | Opening of the Post Office Tower |
| 1966 | Westminster Abbey |
| 1966 | Landscapes |
| 1966 | **1966 World Cup** <br> Stamps to mark England's role as hosts were hastily reissued in August 1966 with ENGLAND WINNERS added. |
| 1966 | British birds |
| 1966 | British technology |
| 1966 | 900th anniversary of the Battle of Hastings |
| 1966 | **Christmas** <br> The first UK Christmas stamps. The idea was championed by Tony Benn and the stamps designed by two 6-year-olds – winners of a Blue Peter competition. |
| 1967 | British wild flowers |
| 1967 | British paintings |
| 1967 | British discoveries and inventions |
| 1967 | Sir Francis Chichester's solo circumnavigation |
| 1968 | British bridges |
| 1969 | Concorde's first flight |

# Sixties TV Gameshows

Gameshows in the sixties were dominated by a few stalwarts, though a few short-lived experimental formats and US adaptions were tried. Without any serious competition, audiences were enormous. How many do you remember watching with your family?

**Call My Bluff**
Almost every episode from the first eight series of Call My Bluff has been wiped from the BBC archives. There were 263 episodes in series one to eight, and only seven episodes still survive.

Face the Music

Just a Minute

Ask the Family

**University Challenge**
Several celebrities appeared on University Challenge before they became famous. These include Stephen Fry, David Starkey, Sebastian Faulks, Julian Fellowes, and Miriam Margolyes (who swore when she answered a question incorrectly). University Challenge has a claim to be the longest running TV quiz show, alongside A Question of Sport.

For Love or Money

**Mr and Mrs**
After watching the Canadian version of Mr and Mrs, Derek Batey was inspired to develop a UK version of the show for Border Television. Batey hosted over 500 episodes, as well as 5,000 on stage after developing a theatrical version.

Play Your Hunch

Take Your Pick

Brain of Britain

**Double Your Money**
A November 1966 episode drew the nation's highest gameshow audience of nearly 20 million viewers.

Exit! It's the Way-Out Show

Many a Slip

Three Little Words

Crossword on 2

# Around the UK

**(25)** Mid twenties: that's adulthood by anybody's reckoning. Were you reading the news, or making it? Here are the national stories that dominated the front pages.

+ Fire on North Sea oil rig Piper Alpha leaves 167 dead
+ Bomb explodes on Pan Am flight over Lockerbie, killing 270
+ Prince Charles avoids Swiss avalanche that kills close friend
+ Loyalists attack IRA funerals at Belfast cemetery
+ 35 dead in Clapham Junction triple-train collision
+ 80,000 honour Nelson Mandela at Wembley Stadium concert (right)
+ Government bans broadcasts of interviews with IRA members
+ SAS officers kill three IRA suspects in Gibraltar
+ Nurses strike in protest over pay and NHS funding
+ Art gallery Tate Liverpool opens
+ New pub laws allow all-day opening in England and Wales
+ Gay rights activists invade BBC News studio
+ Health minister Edwina Curry resigns over egg salmonella scare
+ First killer caught using DNA evidence
+ Dog license scrapped
+ Golfer Sandy Lyle becomes first Briton to win US Masters
+ Celebrity news magazine Hello! first published in UK
+ First BBC Red Nose Day raises £15m for charity
+ Pound note removed from circulation, replaced with £1 coin
+ Seamen at British ports defy union calls to return to work
+ Paddy Ashdown heads new Social and Liberal Democratic Party

*Born this year:*
- World heavyweight champion boxer Tyson Fury born in Manchester
- Singer-songwriter Adele (Adkins) born in Tottenham, London
- Rapper Tinie Tempah born Patrick Chukwuemeka Okogwu in London

*Marx Memorial Library/Mary Evans*

The Nelson Mandela Freedom March used the opportunity of Mandela's 70th birthday to call for his release on a journey from Glasgow to London. Just twenty-five marchers took part each day, one for each year spent in prison by Mandela. The march culminated at the Nelson Mandela Birthday Tribute at a packed Wembley stadium; 600 million more watched the event worldwide. Despite the resistance of the UK and US governments, Nelson Mandela – and his cause – were now the talk of

# The Biggest Hits When You Were 30

How many of these big tunes from the year you turned thirty will still strike a chord decades later?

No Limit ♪ 2 Unlimited
Oh Carolina ♪ Shaggy
Young at Heart ♪ The Bluebells
All That She Wants ♪ Ace of Base
**Dreams ♪ Gabrielle**
Gabrielle wrote Dreams when a woman said, 'This is as good as it is going to get for you,' while the singer was covering Luther Vandross songs in a club.

Pray ♪ Take That
**Living on My Own ♪ Freddie Mercury**
Originally on Mercury's 1985 solo album, Living on My Own was remixed and re-released two years after his death. The video was initially vetoed by the record company because of its perceived promiscuity. It was filmed at Mercury's 39th birthday in 1985.

Mr Vain ♪ Culture Beat
Relight My Fire ♪ Take That with Lulu
**I'd Do Anything for Love ♪ Meat Loaf**
At twelve minutes long, this epic song needed several radio edits to get the maximum airtime (the vocals don't even begin until two minutes into the track). The equally epic video, recreating Beauty and the Beast, was directed by Michael Bay.

**Mr Blobby ♪ Mr Blobby**
Mr Blobby is regularly voted as the most annoying Christmas number one of all time.

Babe ♪ Take That

# ...and the Movies You Saw That Year, Too

From award winners to crowd pleasers, here are the movies that played as your third decade drew to a close.

**Jurassic Park** 🎬 Sam Neill, Jeff Goldblum
During post-production of Jurassic Park, Steven Spielberg was also required to shoot his next picture, Schindler's List – a situation he greatly resented.

The Remains of the Day 🎬 Anthony Hopkins, Emma Thompson
**Groundhog Day** 🎬 Bill Murray, Andie MacDowell
During the car chase scene, Murray was bitten by the groundhog three times.

True Romance 🎬 Christian Slater, Patricia Arquette
The Nightmare Before Christmas 🎬 Chris Sarandon, Catherine O'Hara
**Bram Stoker's Dracula** 🎬 Gary Oldman, Winona Ryder
Oldman hired a voice coach to help him drop his voice an octave to play the titular vampire.

The Piano 🎬 Holly Hunter, Harvey Keitel
Carlito's Way 🎬 Al Pacino, Sean Penn
The Fugitive 🎬 Harrison Ford, Tommy Lee Jones
A Few Good Men 🎬 Tom Cruise, Jack Nicholson
Candyman 🎬 Virginia Madsen, Tony Todd
Hard Boiled 🎬 Chow Yun-Fat, Tony Chiu-Wai Leung
**Reservoir Dogs** 🎬 Tim Roth, Harvey Keitel
Reservoir Dogs was the directorial debut of Quentin Tarantino, who also cast himself in a small role in the film.

What's Love Got to Do with It 🎬 Angela Bassett, Laurence Fishburne
Sleepless in Seattle 🎬 Tom Hanks, Meg Ryan
Last Action Hero 🎬 Arnold Schwarzenegger, F Murray Abraham
Cliffhanger 🎬 Sylvester Stallone, John Lithgow
Raising Cain 🎬 John Lithgow, Lolita Davidovich
Falling Down 🎬 Michael Douglas, Robert Duvall
Alive 🎬 Ethan Hawke, Vincent Spano
Deep Cover 🎬 Laurence Fishburne, Jeff Goldblum
In the Line of Fire 🎬 Clint Eastwood, John Malkovich
Demolition Man 🎬 Sylvester Stallone, Wesley Snipes

# Around the House

Sometimes with a fanfare but often by stealth, inventions and innovations transformed the 20th-century household. Here's what arrived between the ages of 10 and 30.

| | |
|---|---|
| 1973 | BIC lighter |
| 1974 | Sticky notes |
| 1975 | Betamax movies |
| 1976 | **VHS movies**<br>The last film ever released on VHS was David Cronenberg's 2006 thriller, A History of Violence. |
| 1977 | Sony Walkman |
| 1977 | Auto focus cameras |
| 1978 | Electronic (computer-controlled) sewing machines |
| 1978 | Slide Away (sofa) beds |
| 1979 | **Black + Decker DustBuster**<br>Black + Decker came up with the idea of a cordless vacuum while working on a cordless drill for NASA. |
| 1979 | Shake n' Vac |
| 1982 | CD Players |
| 1983 | Dyson bagless vacuum cleaner |
| 1983 | **Nintendo Entertainment System (NES)**<br>Super Mario Bros is the best-selling NES game of all time. |
| 1984 | Sony Discman (changed to CD Walkman in 1999) |
| 1985 | Shower radio |
| 1988 | Sega Megadrive |
| 1989 | Game Boy |
| 1990 | Self-wringing mop<br>The 2015 film Joy was based on Joy Mangano, the creator of the self-wringing mop – the Miracle Mop. |
| 1991 | Memory foam mattresses |
| 1992 | ThighMaster<br>This nineties fad was invented by the heir to the Reynolds Tobacco company. Six million were sold through celebrity endorsement. |
| 1993 | Colour Catcher (run prevention washing sheets) |

# British Prime Ministers in Your Lifetime

These are the occupants of 10 Downing Street, London, during your lifetime, not including Larry the resident cat. Don't be deceived by that unassuming, black, blast-proof door: Number 10 features a warren of more than 100 rooms.

| | |
|---|---|
| 1957–63 | **Harold Macmillan**<br>Macmillan was the scion of a wealthy publishing family, but the biggest secret of his life was kept under wraps: his wife Dorothy's 30-year affair with fellow Conservative (and Krays associate) Robert Boothby. Macmillan died aged 92; his last words were, 'I think I will go to sleep now.' |
| 1963–64 | Sir Alec Douglas-Home |
| 1964–70 | Harold Wilson |
| 1970–74 | Edward Heath |
| 1974–76 | Harold Wilson |
| 1976–79 | James Callaghan |
| 1979–90 | **Margaret Thatcher**<br>'Today we were unlucky,' said the chilling statement from the IRA, 'but remember we only have to be lucky once.' The 1994 bombing of the Grand hotel in Brighton may not have killed the prime minister, but five others died and others were left with lifelong injuries. |
| 1990–97 | John Major |
| 1997–2007 | Tony Blair |
| 2007–10 | **Gordon Brown**<br>Brown has no sight in his left eye after being kicked in a school rugby game. |
| 2010–16 | David Cameron |
| 2016–19 | **Theresa May**<br>Asked in a pre-election interview about the naughtiest thing she'd ever done, May said that she'd once run through a field of wheat with her friends. |
| 2019–22 | Boris Johnson |
| 2022 | Liz Truss |
| 2022– | Rishi Sunak |

# Shopping When You Were Born

In 1947, the government calculated inflation for the first time using a basket of frequently purchased goods. This list has been reviewed ever since; the changes mirror our ever-changing tastes and habits. Here's what housewives were buying when you were small.

Sliced white bread
Chocolate coated biscuits
Dry cleaning
**Potato crisps**
Crisps entered the basket of goods in 1962, the same year Golden Wonder (bought by Imperial Tobacco) launched cheese and onion flavoured crisps. Golden Wonder, Smith's and soon Walkers fought for the market, and consumption rocketed.

Oven ready chicken
Cuts of halibut
Second-hand car
Welfare milk scheme
Ground coffee
**Frozen croquettes**
As more homes had freezers and the desire for ready meals increased, frozen food was all the rage. Frozen croquettes were released in the early 1960s and were a resounding success.

**Canned fruit salad**
Canned fruit salad was designed to use the fruit scraps that couldn't be used in canning. Fruit salad arrived in the 1940s and became one of the most popular canned fruits available. You could even use it to make a fruit salad cake.

TV set rental
Gloss paint
Ceiling paper
Jeans
Latex backed carpet
Refrigerator
Ready-made suit
**Terylene slacks**
Created in Manchester in 1941, Terylene revolutionised clothing in the 1950s. It was used by Mary Quant to make the original miniskirts, and Ray Davies of The Kinks advertised it.

# Popular Food in the 1970s

Jump into the next decade and it's time to roll out the hostess trolley. If it's not highly processed, artificially coloured, moulded and served in a novelty dish, is it even food? Still, most of it went down very well with the kids – and still does today, given half a chance.

Lemon meringue pie

Cheese and pineapple

**Black Forest Gâteau**

The Black Forest Gâteau is named after the kirsch alcohol made from Black Forest sour cherries, rather than the Black Forest region in Germany.

Dream Topping

Mateus Rose, Liebfraumilch and Chianti

**Cornetto**

Cornetto cones were created by Spica, an Italian ice-cream company, in 1976. The company was bought by Unilever not long after, who then marketed the dessert in Europe.

Quavers

**Quiche**

Unlike the gâteau above, quiche Lorraine *was* named after the area in which it was created. It is considered a French dish, even though Lorraine was under German rule at the time.

**Pot Noodle**

The original Pot Noodle made in 1979 did not contain a sauce sachet – these were only added in 1992.

Fondue

Smash

Scampi in a basket

Banoffee pie

**Chili con carne**

Chili is the state dish of Texas, where many people think the recipe originated. Before WWII, hundreds of individual parlours all insisted they had their own secret recipe.

Prawn cocktails

Profiteroles

The Full English Breakfast

# Beer of the Seventies

You could haul a seven-pint tin of Watneys Party Seven to a celebration. Someone would be drinking bland Watneys Red, or Courage Tavern ('It's what your right arm's for'). But how about a drop of that cold, refreshing lager you tried on holiday? 'Mine's a pint!' said millions of Brits.

Watneys Party Seven

Whitbread Tankard

Watneys Red

Double Diamond

### Carlsberg

The inventor of Carlsberg, JC Jacobsen, gave a Ted Talk on his life philosophy in 2017 – 130 years after he died. He was brought back to life via hologram and even fielded questions from the audience.

### Heineken

The Heineken International company owns more than 250 other brands, many of which you'll probably recognise such as Amstel, Desperados and Strongbow.

Tennant's Gold Label

### Guinness

When Arthur Guinness started his now-famous business he rented an unused brewery on a 9,000-year lease – though the contract was eventually voided when the company bought the land and surrounding areas to expand the business.

Worthington E

Carling Black Label

Harp

Stella Artois

Ind Coope Super

Younger's Scotch Ale

Bass Charrington

### Strongbow

HP Bulmer named his drink after one of the greatest knights in English history, Richard de Clare, who was given the nickname Strongbow.

Long Life

# Seventies TV Gameshows

With light entertainment increasingly becoming the bedrock of TV channel success, the seventies saw an explosion of formats from gimmicks to US imports. Which ones got you shouting at the telly?

### It's a Knockout
Although this show began in 1966 and it limped on into the new century, the seventies was It's a Knockout's golden age, thanks in no small part to presenter Stuart Hall. The winning teams proceeded to represent the UK at the European final, Jeux Sans Frontières.

I'm Sorry I Haven't a Clue

Jokers Wild

My Music

### A Question of Sport
A Question of Sport is the world's longest running TV sports quiz. The first episode was recorded in 1970 in a converted chapel in Rusholme, Manchester, and the show is still recorded in the city as it surpasses 1,300 episodes.

Quote... Unquote

Whodunnit?

Mastermind

Screen Test

### Celebrity Squares
Inspired by the game noughts and crosses, Celebrity Squares was based on the US gameshow Hollywood Squares. The original run was presented by Bob Monkhouse, who also returned to host the revival of the show in the 1990s.

Gambit

The Generation Game

The Golden Shot

The Indoor League

Password

Runaround

Sale of the Century

The Sky's the Limit

Winner Takes All

# Popular Boys' Names

**40**

Just as middle age crept up unnoticed, so the most popular names also evolved. The traditional choices – possibly including yours – were fast losing their appeal to new parents.

**Jack**
This is Jack's eighth year on top. He'll remain the nation's first choice from 1996 to 2008.

Joshua
Thomas
James
Daniel
Oliver
Benjamin
Samuel
William
Joseph
Harry
Matthew
Lewis
Luke
Ethan
George
Alfie
Adam
Callum
Alexander
Mohammed
Ryan
Cameron
Charlie
Connor
Ben

**Rising and falling stars:**
While names fell in and out of fashion in great numbers in the eighties and nineties, the pace has slowed. New this year: Logan, Spencer, Noah, Jude and Luca. Out: Josh, Anthony and Marcus.

# Popular Girls' Names

It's a similar story for girls' names. Increasing numbers took their infant inspiration from popular culture. The worlds of music, film and now the internet are all fertile hunting grounds for those in need of inspiration.

**Emily**
Having spent six years as the bridesmaid to Chloe's bride, Emily takes the top spot for two years. Only since 2019 has she finally slipped from the top 10.

Ellie
Chloe
Jessica
Sophie
Megan
Lucy
Olivia
Charlotte
Hannah
Katie
Ella
Holly
Grace
Mia
Amy
Lauren
Molly
Emma
Abigail
Amelia
Caitlin
Lily
Bethany
Rebecca
Georgia

**Rising and falling stars:**
Summer, Tegan and Faith: welcome to the Top 100!
Katherine, Samantha, Yasmin and Aaliyah: we're afraid your time is up.

# F1 Champions

If you fancy your chances in Formula One, start young. Sebastian Vettel won at 23. *El Maestro*, Juan Manuel Fangio, is the oldest winner to date, at 46. The field is wide open for an older champ, right?

Alain Prost 🏆 (1985-6,89,93)
**Nelson Piquet** 🏆 (1981,83,87)
Nelson Piquet lost his civilian driving licence in 2007 due to numerous speeding and parking offences. He was ordered to attend a week of lessons and pass an exam.

**Ayrton Senna** 🏆 (1988,90-1)
Two days before Senna's fatal crash at Imola, he was early to the scene of a near-fatal crash for Rubens Barrichello. One day before, he inspected the car of Roland Ratzenberger as the mortally-injured Austrian was taken to hospital – the same facility that would attempt to save Senna's life the following day after his crash on the same corner. An Austrian flag was later found in Senna's cockpit, intended to be unfurled as a tribute to Ratzenberger.

Nigel Mansell 🏆 (1992)
**Michael Schumacher** 🏆 (1994-5,2000-04)
Michael Schumacher was one of a handful of drivers to appear as themselves in the Pixar film Cars, voicing a Ferrari F430.

Damon Hill 🏆 (1996)
Jacques Villeneuve 🏆 (1997)
Mika Häkkinen 🏆 (1998-99)
Fernando Alonso 🏆 (2005-6)
A Fernando Alonso Sports Complex in Spain includes a museum dedicated to Alonso, a karting circuit, and a golf course.

Kimi Räikkönen 🏆 (2007)
Lewis Hamilton 🏆 (2008,14-15,17-20)
Jenson Button 🏆 (2009)

# Fashion in the Seventies

The decade that taste forgot? Or a kickback against the sixties and an explosion of individuality? Skirts got shorter (and longer). Block colours and peasant chic vied with sequins and disco glamour. How many of your seventies outfits would you still wear today?

Flares
Platform shoes
**Laura Ashley**
While working as a secretary, Laura Ashley was inspired to produce printed fabric after seeing a display at the Victoria and Albert Museum. Struggling to make a profit, Laura Ashley and her husband and children once lived in tents in Wales for six months.

Gucci
Diane Von Furstenberg
Tie Dye
**Kaftans**
Brought to western culture via the hippie trail, the kaftan's popularity was boosted further when Elizabeth Taylor wore a kaftan-inspired dress for her second wedding to Richard Burton in 1975.

Liza Minnelli
Lurex and suede
David Bowie
Afro, braids or a perm
Jumpsuit
Sequin hot pants
Moon boots
**Double denim**
Double denim garnered the nickname the 'Canadian tuxedo' after Bing Crosby was refused entry to a hotel in Vancouver because he wore a denim ensemble. Levi subsequently designed Crosby a denim tuxedo.

**Vivienne Westwood**
Previously a primary school teacher, Vivienne Westwood lived in an ex-council flat in Clapham until 2000. Her son from her relationship with Malcolm McLaren founded lingerie brand Agent Provocateur.

# Shopping in 1970

Frozen foods and eating out swallow up an increasingly larger share of the family budget in the seventies. Or how about a day trip (don't forget your AA membership and your mac), then home for a sweet sherry?

Frozen chicken

Mushrooms

Frozen beans

**Sherry**

Sherry consumption peaked in the UK in the 1970s following the development of sweet versions – often using added syrups or sugars – known as creams and developed for British palates.

Night storage heater

Plastic Mackintosh

**MOT test**

Introduced in 1960, the MOT was designed to test the brakes, lights, and steering of all vehicles over 10 years old. This was progressively reduced to every three years by 1967, and the test changed to include tyres.

State school meal

Canteen meal

**Cup of tea**

The 1970s saw a significant increase in eating out, so a cup of tea was added to the basket. Despite Britain's reputation as tea lovers, coffee sales overtook tea sales for the first time in 1986.

Cafe sandwich

**Local authority rent**

Local authority rent was added to the basket of goods in the 1970s; by 1979, 42% of Britons lived in council homes.

Paper handkerchiefs

Auto association subs

Keg of ale

Fresh cream

**Gammon**

While gammon gained popularity during the 1970s due to its unlikely pairing with pineapple rings, the word 'gammon' is now also used as an insult towards the political right, coined in response to 'snowflake'.

# Post-war Chocolate

You'll find nearly all of these on the supermarket shelves, even though the most recently invented chocolate bar here was brought to market thirty years ago. Gulp.

| | |
|---|---|
| 1948 | Fudge |
| 1951 | **Bounty**<br>If you wanted to sell a chocolate bar with curved ends and swirls on the top, in theory there's nothing that maker Mars could do to stop you: the shape was decreed not distinctive enough to trademark in 2009. Do check with a lawyer first, though. |
| 1957 | Munchies |
| 1958 | Picnic |
| 1962 | **After Eight Mint Chocolate Thins**<br>A billion of these are churned out every year (although we've never heard anyone call them chocolate thins). |
| 1962 | Topic |
| 1963 | Toffee Crisp |
| 1967 | Twix |
| 1970 | Chomp |
| 1970 | Curly Wurly |
| 1973 | Freddo |
| 1976 | **Double Decker**<br>Double Deckers contain raisins, don't they? Not any more: they were removed from the recipe during the eighties. |
| 1976 | Starbar |
| 1976 | **Yorkie**<br>'It's not for girls,' said the adverts. The sexist marketing of Yorkie reached its peak – or trough – in 2005 with special pink editions. By 2011 the complaints outweighed the commercial advantage. The 'men only' angle was dropped. |
| 1978 | Lion Bar |
| 1980 | Drifter |
| 1983 | **Wispa**<br>For twenty years, Wispa was the go-to Aero alternative. But then in 2003 it was gone. A predictable outcry followed and in 2007 it was back on the shelves. Phew. |
| 1992 | Time Out |

# Books of the Decade

Family, friends, TV, and more: there are as many midlife distractions as there are books on the shelf. Did you get drawn in by these bestsellers, all published in your thirties?

| | |
|---|---|
| 1993 | The Shipping News by E Annie Proulx |
| 1993 | Birdsong by Sebastian Faulks |
| 1993 | Paddy Clarke Ha Ha Ha by Roddy Doyle |
| 1994 | A Suitable Boy by Vikram Seth |
| 1994 | Snow Falling on Cedars by David Guterson |
| 1995 | A Fine Balance by Rohinton Mistry |
| 1996 | Infinite Jest by David Foster Wallace |
| 1996 | **A Game of Thrones by George RR Martin**<br>The idea for the story came to Martin as a child through his pet turtles. They lived in a toy castle, and he pretended they were kings, lords and knights. |
| 1996 | Bridget Jones's Diary by Helen Fielding |
| 1997 | **Harry Potter And The Philosopher's Stone by J K Rowling**<br>In the film of the book, Rik Mayall played the part of Peeves the Poltergeist. The scene was cut before release. |
| 1997 | American Pastoral by Philip Roth |
| 1997 | The God of Small Things by Arundhati Roy |
| 1997 | Underworld by Don DeLillo |
| 1997 | Memoirs of a Geisha by Arthur Golden |
| 1997 | Blindness by José Saramago |
| 1998 | The Poisonwood Bible by Barbara Kingsolver |
| 1999 | Disgrace by J M Coetzee |
| 1999 | Being Dead by Jim Crace |
| 1999 | Ghostwritten by David Mitchell |
| 2000 | White Teeth by Zadie Smith |
| 2000 | The Blind Assassin by Margaret Atwood |
| 2001 | Atonement by Ian McEwan |
| 2001 | The Corrections by Jonathan Franzen |
| 2001 | Austerlitz by W G Sebald |
| 2001 | Life of Pi by Yann Martel |
| 2002 | Everything Is Illuminated by Jonathan Safran Foer |
| 2002 | The Lovely Bones by Alice Sebold |

# TV Newsreaders: The Early Days

Trusted, familiar, and mostly with received pronunciation: these are the faces that brought you and your family the news, and the dates they shuffled their papers.

**Richard Baker** 📺 (1954-82)
In 1954, Baker introduced the BBC's first TV news broadcast. Seventies children know his voice as the narrator of Mary, Mungo and Midge.

Robert Dougall 📺 (1955-73)
Kenneth Kendall 📺 (1955-69)
**Angela Rippon** 📺 (1975-2002)
The UK's first regular female newsreader and known nationwide for her 1976 Morecambe and Wise appearance.

**Jill Dando** 📺 (1988-99)
The shocking murder of Dando on her doorstep in 1999 remains unsolved.

Moira Stuart 📺 (1981-2007)
**Peter Woods** 📺 (1964-81)
Woods is the biological father of BBC journalist and presenter Justin Webb.

**Nan Winton** 📺 (1960-61)
Winton was the BBC's first on-screen female newsreader in a shortlived 1960 trial deemed unacceptable by viewers.

Reginald Bosanquet 📺 (1967-79)
Michael Aspel 📺 (1960-68)
Corbet Woodall 📺 (1963-67)
Anna Ford 📺 (1976-2006)
Jan Leeming 📺 (1980-87)
Lynette Lithgow 📺 (1988-96)
Selina Scott 📺 (1980-86)
**Sue Lawley** 📺 (1981-88)
Alongside her news duties, Lawley is best known for her 18-year stint presenting BBC Four's Desert Island Discs. She left the role in 2006.

Julia Somerville 📺 (1983-99)

# Cars of the 1970s

How did you get around in the seventies? Was it in one of the decade's fancy new Range Rovers, or perhaps something more modest like a Morris Marina? Here are the decade's most famous (and infamous) cars.

Ford Capri

Vauxhall HC Viva

**Ford Escort**

Introduced in 1968, the Ford Escort went on to be the best-selling car in Britain in the 1980s and 1990s. The car was brought back into the spotlight in 2013, when it was featured in Fast & Furious 6.

Jaguar XJ

Triumph TR7

Austin Allegro

**Austin Maxi**

The Austin Maxi was the first British five-door hatchback, and one of the first cars to be featured on the BBC's Wheelbase show.

Ford Cortina

**Ford Granada**

Designed as a European executive car, the Granada was popular for taxi and police car use. It was also modified for use as a hearse and limousine, and was often seen in The Sweeney.

Leyland Princess

Triumph Dolomite

Vauxhall Cavalier

Range Rover

**Morris Marina**

The popular Morris Marina is ranked amongst the worst cars ever built. The car was released with poor suspension, chronic understeer, and windscreen wipers fitted the wrong way round.

Hillman Avenger

Saab 99

Datsun Sunny

BMW 316

**Volkswagen Beetle**

Affectionately known as the bug in English-speaking countries, it is called turtle in Bolivia, frog in Indonesia, and hunchback in Poland.

# Shopping in 1980

Mortgage interest rates were around 15% as we went into the eighties, not much lower as we left, and added to our basket in 1980. If you had any money left over perhaps you were spending it on home perms, cement and lamb's liver!

Lamb's liver

**Tea bags**
Tea is one of the few items included in the basket since the start. Tea bags were added in 1980; loose tea was removed in 2002.

**Smash**
Smash sales soared following the 1974 TV adverts featuring the Smash Martians. It was replaced in 1987 by oven chips.

Cider

Wine

Mortgage Interest

White spirit

Cement

Toilet seat

Electric plug

**Colour TV**
Colour TV sets outnumbered black and white sets in 1976.

Record player

**Cassette recorder**
Cassette recorders were first introduced by Philips in the 1960s and were originally intended for dictation and journalists.

Electric hairdryer

Carpet sweeper

Continental quilt

Drycell batteries

Colour photo film

Briefcase

Home perm

**National Trust fees**
Membership to the National Trust significantly increased throughout the 1980s (around 5.6 million people are members today). The Giant's Causeway is the most visited national attraction.

# Olympic Medallists in Your Life

With seven gold medals, Jason Kenny is without equal while the unique achievements of Laura Trott – now Mrs Kenny – brings the household tally to twelve. Meanwhile, over at the Paralympics, swimmer-cyclist Sarah Storey has an incredible 17 gold medals. And medals of all colours? Here are the heroes of Team GB at the Summer Olympics.

Jason Kenny (9) 🏅 Cycling
**Bradley Wiggins (8)** 🏅 Cycling
Britain's most decorated Olympian until Kenny took the crown in Tokyo, Wiggo acquired various nicknames throughout his career. In France he was referred to as 'Le Gentleman', while the Dutch apparently called him 'The Banana with the Sideburns'.

**Chris Hoy (7)** 🏅 Cycling
**Laura Kenny (6)** 🏅 Cycling
Our most successful female Olympian with five gold medals, Trott (now Kenny) began life with a collapsed lung and asthma.

Steve Redgrave (6) 🏅 Rowing
Max Whitlock (6) 🏅 Gymnastics
Charlotte Dujardin (6) 🏅 Equestrianism
**Ben Ainslie (5)** 🏅 Sailing
Known for his hot temper, Ben Ainslie has accused competitors of teaming up against him. He was disqualified from the world championships in Australia for confronting a photographer who Ainslie felt had impeded his progress.

Adam Peaty (5) 🏅 Swimming
**Katherine Grainger (5)** 🏅 Rowing
Grainger is the first British woman to win medals at five successive Olympic games, from Sydney to Rio.

Mo Farah (4) 🏅 Athletics
Matthew Pinsent (4) 🏅 Rowing
Ed Clancy (4) 🏅 Cycling
Ian Stark (4) 🏅 Equestrianism
Louis Smith (4) 🏅 Gymnastics
Becky Adlington (4) 🏅 Swimming
Seb Coe (4) 🏅 Athletics
Ginny Leng (4) 🏅 Equestrianism

It's striking that our most decorated Olympians did so in recent decades. Of the 18 athletes earning four medals or more since you were born, Seb Coe came off the starting blocks first: he won his first medal at the 1980 Moscow Olympics at the age of 23 (shortly after breaking the 1,000 metre record in Oslo, above).

Run the slide rule over every modern Olympics, starting in 1896, and only six more GB athletes have achieved the same phenomenal success.

# Winter Olympics Venues Since You Were Born

Unless you're an athlete or winter sports fan, the Winter Olympics can slip past almost unnoticed. These are the venues; can you remember the host countries and years?

Lillehammer
Salt Lake City
Sapporo
**Albertville**
The last Games to be held in the same year as the Summer Olympics, with the next Winter Olympics held two years later.

Turin
Grenoble
Beijing
Sarajevo
Lake Placid
Sochi
**Innsbruck (twice)**
This usually snowy city experienced its mildest winter in 60 years; the army was called in to transport snow and ice from the mountains. Nevertheless, twelve years later, the Winter Olympics were back.

Nagano
Calgary
Vancouver
PyeongChang

The answers are upside down at the bottom.

**Answers:** *Lillehammer: Norway, 1994; Salt Lake City: USA, 2002; Sapporo: Japan, 1972; Albertville: France, 1992; Turin: Italy, 2006; Grenoble: France, 1968; Beijing: China, 2022; Sarajevo: Yugoslavia, 1984; Lake Placid: USA, 1980; Sochi: Russia, 2014; Innsbruck: Austria, 1964; Nagano: Japan, 1998; Calgary: Canada, 1988; Innsbruck: Austria, 1976; Vancouver: Canada, 2010; PyeongChang: South Korea, 2018*

# Fashion in the Eighties

Eighties fashion was many things, but subtle wasn't one of them. Brash influences were everywhere from aerobics to Wall Street, from pop princesses to preppy polo shirts. The result was chaotic, but fun. How many eighties throwbacks still lurk in your closet?

Shoulder pads or puffed sleeves

### Scrunchies
Patented in 1987 by nightclub singer Rommy Revson, the first scrunchie was designed using the waistband of her pyjama bottoms. The softer alternative to hair bands was named after Revson's dog Scunchie (no, that's not a typo).

### Conical bras
Inspired by 1950s bullet bras, Jean Paul Gaultier introduced the cone bra in 1984. As a child he fashioned the bra for his teddy bear; years later he reworked the look for Madonna's Blonde Ambition tour in 1990.

Acid wash jeans

### Slogan t-shirts
Designer Katharine Hamnett introduced slogan t-shirts, famously revealing one displaying an anti-nuclear statement when meeting Margaret Thatcher in 1984. Wham opted for 'Choose Life'; for Frankie Goes to Hollywood it was 'Frankie Says Relax'.

### Leotards and leg-warmers
Leg-warmers reached the masses following the release of Fame and Flashdance, as well as Jane Fonda exercise videos. Nowadays, leg-warmers are even worn by babies while they have their nappies changed.

Deely boppers, bangle earrings or a polka dot hair bow
Pedal pushers or leggings
Guyliner
Levi 501s
Pixie boots
Ra-ra skirt and PVC belts

### Dr Martens
Dr Martens were designed by a German soldier to aid the recovery of his broken foot. Pete Townshend of The Who was the first rock star to wear the boots on stage, and the shoe was adopted by numerous subcultures.

# Grand Designs

Governments around the world spent much of the 20th century nation building (and rebuilding). Here is a selection of striking civil engineering achievements between the ages of 0 and 40.

| | |
|---|---|
| 1965 | Mont Blanc Tunnel, France & Italy |
| 1965 | Zeeland Bridge, Netherlands |
| 1966 | **Almondsbury Interchange, Bristol & Gloucester**<br>The Almondsbury Interchange was the first example of a four-level stack in the UK, and remains one of only three of its kind in the country. |
| 1967 | **Second Blackwall Tunnel, London**<br>The second Blackwall tunnel is relatively straight, unlike the first which is curved. That was to avoid a sewer, but also reportedly so that horses (the main means of transport when built) didn't see daylight at the other end and bolt. |
| 1969 | Humber Refinery, Northern Lincolnshire |
| 1970 | Aswan Dam, Aswan |
| 1970 | Hyde Park Barracks, London |
| 1971 | **Spaghetti Junction, Birmingham**<br>Officially the Gravelly Hill Interchange, Spaghetti Junction was named by the Guinness Book of World Records as 'the most complex interchange on the British road system'. |
| 1973 | Bosphorus Bridge, Istanbul |
| 1976 | **Sonnenberg Tunnel, Lucerne**<br>A 5,000 ft road tunnel that was built to double up as a nuclear shelter for up to 20,000 people. Blast doors at the entrance weigh 350 tons...but take 24 hours to close. |
| 1981 | Humber Bridge, Kingston upon Hull |
| 1982 | Thames Barrier, London |
| 1984 | Kylesku Bridge, Scotland (Drochaid a' Chaolais Chumhaing) |
| 1989 | Grande Arche, Paris |
| 1994 | **Channel Tunnel, UK & France**<br>Although construction started in 1988, the idea of a tunnel between the two countries goes back to the 1800s, and Napoleon supported the idea. The tunnel was recognised as one of the 'Seven Wonders of the Modern World' by the American Society of Civil Engineers. |

# World Buildings

Buildings that are known the world over for all the right (and the wrong) reasons and were opened before you turned 50.

| 1968 | Madison Square Garden, New York City, New York |
| 1969 | John Hancock Center, Chicago |
| 1973 | Sears Tower, Chicago, Illinois |
| 1973 | World Trade Center, New York |
| 1973 | **Sydney Opera House, Sydney** |

1973    **Sydney Opera House, Sydney**
The estimated cost for the construction was AU$7m (£4m). It ended up costing AU$102m (£59m), and took 14 years to build rather than the four years planned.

| 1976 | CN Tower, Toronto |
| 1977 | Pompidou Centre, Paris |
| 1981 | Sydney Tower, Sydney |
| 1990 | Washington National Cathedral, Washington DC |

1983    **Trump Tower, New York**
How many floors there are in Trump Tower? An easy question, right? It was built with 58 floors. But Trump wasn't happy… the ceilings are high on some floors, so the numbers jump from the 6th to the 13th floor. Now it has 68!

| 1988 | Parliament House, Canberra |
| 1989 | Louvre Pyramid, Paris |
| 1996 | Petronas Twin Towers, Kuala Lampur |

1997    **Guggenheim Museum, Bilbao**
Bilbao saw a surge in economic growth following the museum's opening. The 'Bilbao effect' is now the name for the positive local impact a building can instigate.

| 1999 | Burj Al Arab, Dubai |
| 2000 | Emirates Tower One, Dubai |
| 2007 | Heydar Aliyev Center, Baku |
| 2008 | Atlantis, The Palm, Dubai |

2010    **Burj Khalifa, Dubai**
At half a mile high, it's the world's tallest building and freestanding structure.

# Shopping in 1987

The shelves, fridges and freezers are piled high with convenience foods. What did we do with all that extra time we'd saved? First, dig out the indigestion tablets. Then tackle a spot of DIY and finally move house, it seems!

**Squash racket**
The classic eighties sport. Prince Philip played squash to relax while Queen Elizabeth II was in labour with Prince Charles.

Muesli

Spaghetti

Jam doughnuts

Swiss roll

Beefburgers

Mince

Garlic sausage

Frozen prawns

Brie

**Red Leicester**
Originally called Leicestershire Cheese, the cheese was renamed Red Leicester after World War II to differentiate it from 'White Leicester' made during rationing when the use of colouring agents was banned.

Conifer

Frozen curry and rice

**Fish and chips**
Synonymous with British cuisine and described by Winston Churchill as 'the good companions', fish and chips were exempt from rationing during World War II, as the government feared any limitations would damage the morale of the nation.

VHS recorder

Ready mixed filler

**Home telephone**
The popularity of mobile phones has led to a decrease of landlines. Only 73% of British households had a landline used to make calls in 2020.

Fabric conditioner

Estate agent fees

Indigestion tablets

# Books of the Decade

By our forties, most of us have decided what we like to read. But occasionally a book can break the spell, revealing the delights of other genres. Did any of these newly published books do that for you?

| | |
|---|---|
| 2003 | The Kite Runner by Khaled Hosseini |
| 2003 | Vernon God Little by DBC Pierre |
| 2003 | Brick Lane by Monica Ali |
| 2004 | The Line of Beauty by Alan Hollinghurst |
| 2004 | Cloud Atlas by David Mitchell |
| 2004 | Gilead by Marilynne Robinson |
| 2004 | Small Island by Andrea Levy |
| 2005 | Never Let Me Go by Kazuo Ishiguro |
| 2005 | The Book Thief by Markus Zusak |
| 2005 | The Sea by John Banville |
| 2005 | **The Girl with the Dragon Tattoo by Stieg Larsson**<br>Larsson died before the first three books in the series were published. Larsson's partner has a partially completed fourth book – but not the rights to publish it. |
| 2005 | No Country for Old Men by Cormac McCarthy |
| 2005 | Saturday by Ian McEwan |
| 2006 | The Road by Cormac McCarthy |
| 2007 | A Thousand Splendid Suns by Khaled Hosseini |
| 2007 | The Ghost by Robert Harris |
| 2008 | The White Tiger by Aravind Adiga |
| 2008 | **The Hunger Games by Suzanne Collins**<br>The myth of Theseus and the Minotaurs inspired Collins to write The Hunger Games. She didn't intend to write a trilogy but felt compelled to continue the story. |
| 2009 | Wolf Hall by Hilary Mantel |
| 2009 | The Help by Kathryn Stockett |
| 2010 | The Hand That First Held Mine by Maggie O'Farrell |
| 2010 | The Finkler Question by Howard Jacobson |
| 2011 | **Fifty Shades of Grey by EL James**<br>Originally self-published as Twilight fan fiction. |
| 2011 | A Dance with Dragons by George RR Martin |
| 2012 | Gone Girl by Gillian Flynn |

# US Vice Presidents in Your Lifetime

The linchpin of a successful presidency, a springboard to become POTUS, or both? Here are the men – and the woman – who have shadowed the most powerful person in the world in your lifetime. (President in brackets.)

| | |
|---|---|
| 1963-65 | *None*: following the asassination of President Kennedy, Vice President Lyndon Johnson took his place; with no means to fill the vacancy, the office of VP was left vacant. |
| 1965-69 | **Hubert Humphrey** (Lyndon Johnson)<br>Christmas 1977: with just weeks to live, the former VP made goodbye calls. One was to Richard Nixon, the man who had beaten Humphrey to become president in 1968. Sensing Nixon's unhappiness at his status as Washington outcast, Humphrey invited him to take a place of honour at the funeral he knew was fast approaching. |
| 1969-73 | **Spiro Agnew (right)** |
| 1973-74 | Gerald Ford |
| 1974-77 | Nelson Rockefeller |
| 1977-81 | Walter Mondale |
| 1981-89 | **George HW Bush**<br>He is only the second vice president to win the presidency while holding the office of vice president. |
| 1989-93 | **Dan Quayle**<br>You say potato, Quayle said potatoe: he famously told a student to add an 'e' during a 1992 school visit. |
| 1993-2001 | **Al Gore**<br>Gore won the Nobel Peace Prize in 2007. Two others have won: Teddy Roosevelt (1906) and Charles Dawes (1925). |
| 2001-09 | Dick Cheney |
| 2009-17 | Joe Biden |
| 2017-20 | **Mike Pence**<br>In the 90s, Pence took a break from politics to become a conservative radio talk show and television host. |
| 2020- | **Kamala Harris**<br>Harris is the highest-ranked woman in US history and the first woman of colour to hold the office of Vice President. 'While I may be the first woman in this office, I will not be the last,' she said. |

Spiro Agnew resigned in 1973, the second VP to quit in America's history (the first was John Calhoun in 1932). He stepped down after being charged with tax evasion and taking bribes. He covered his legal debts with a loan from friend Frank Sinatra. In 1983, Agnew was compelled to repay $268,000: the money he had taken in bribes, plus interest.

# Stamps in the Seventies

By the seventies, any hobbyist intent on keeping a complete ongoing collection needed deep pockets (or a rich uncle). New stamps were churned out several times a year and the subjects became ever more esoteric: not just flowers and trees but racket sports, or paintings of horse races. Was your album gathering dust by then?

| | |
|---|---|
| 1970 | Commonwealth Games |
| 1971 | British rural architecture |
| 1972 | Polar explorers |
| 1972 | Village churches |
| 1972 | Royal Silver Wedding celebration |
| 1973 | Plant a Tree Year |
| 1973 | County Cricket |
| 1973 | **400th anniversary of the birth of Inigo Jones** <br> Not a household name by today's standards, Jones was an early and influential architect. He designed Covent Garden Square and parts of St Paul's Cathedral. |
| 1973 | Royal Wedding (Princess Anne and Mark Phillips) |
| 1973 | Britain's entry into the EC |
| 1974 | Medieval Warriors |
| 1975 | Sailing |
| 1975 | 100 years since the birth of Jane Austen |
| 1976 | 100 years of the telephone |
| 1976 | **British cultural traditions** <br> The four chosen were a Morris dancer, a Scots piper, a Welsh harpist and an Archdruid. |
| 1977 | Racket sports |
| 1977 | Silver Jubilee |
| 1977 | Wildlife |
| 1978 | **Energy resources** <br> In an era before renewable energy the choices made were oil, coal, natural gas and electricity. |
| 1978 | Horses |
| 1979 | Dogs |
| 1979 | Spring wild flowers |
| 1979 | Paintings of horse races |
| 1979 | 150 years of the Metropolitan Police |

# More Things People Do Now...

... that nobody ever did when you were small – because they couldn't, wouldn't, or definitely shouldn't!

✦ **Place a bet *during* a sporting event**
This became popular in the 1990s; first on the phone, now online.

✦ Turn on underfloor heating

✦ **Buy soft toilet rolls**
In 1942, a wonder was created in Walthamstow's St Andrews Road, one for which the bottoms of the world owe a huge debt: two-ply, soft toilet roll ('It's splinter-free'!). It was christened Andrex.

✦ Talk to a smart speaker

✦ Clean up dog poo (not doing it has been an offence since 1996)

✦ Listen to a podcast

✦ **Do a Sudoku puzzle**
How many Japanese words do you know? Tsunami? Karaoke? Sake? In 2005, you likely added another: Sudoku (meaning 'single number'). The puzzle originated in the USA – but was popularised by Wayne Gould, a Hong Kong judge from New Zealand who found a translated version in a Tokyo bookshop.

✦ **Cheat in a pub quiz**
Which two capital cities mean the same in different languages? Who knows? Google knows, and a quick trip to the loo (phone in hand) is a modern phenomenon. (The answer is Sierra Leone's Freetown and Gabon's Libreville – but of course you knew that.)

✦ Order something for same day delivery

✦ Use chopsticks

✦ Fly a drone

✦ **Never watch live TV**
Owning a TV but not watching any live programmes (just streamed content) might sound odd. But that is the reality for many – and around 1.5m have ditched the TV completely.

✦ Eat in the street

✦ Buy water

✦ **Use SatNav**
In the 1980s, Ronald Reagan permitted civilian use of satellites for navigation and opened up a world in which we never need to get lost again – unless we want to. Or the USA pulls the plug.

✦ Argue for hours with strangers you'll never meet

# A Lifetime of Progress

It's easy to lose sight of the breadth and pace of life-enhancing inventions made as you grew up – although some of these didn't stand the test of time! These are the biggies before you turned 50.

| | |
|---|---|
| 1988 | **Internet virus**<br>The first Internet worm (ie self-replicating) was designed to go after passwords. Its inventor was the son of the man who invented... computer passwords. |
| 1989 | World Wide Web |
| 1990 | Hubble space telescope |
| 1991 | Websites |
| 1992 | Digital hand-sized mobile phone |
| 1994 | Bluetooth |
| 1995 | **Mouse with scroll wheel**<br>Mouse scroll wheels were developed for large Excel sheets but soon became used as a means of scrolling any content. |
| 1996 | DVD player |
| 1997 | WebTV |
| 1998 | Google |
| 1999 | Wi-Fi |
| 2000 | Camera phone |
| 2001 | **Wikipedia**<br>Initially intended to be written by experts, around two dozen articles were written in the first year, so Wikipedia was opened up for anyone to edit. Around 5 million articles in English now await the curious, with many more in languages from Swedish to Tagalog. Little surprise that one article is a list of lists of lists. |
| 2004 | Facebook |
| 2007 | **Apple iPhone**<br>The top-secret development of the iPhone began in 2004 under the code name 'Project Purple'. It was announced at a convention by Steve Jobs in 2007 at 9:41am; that's why iPhone adverts show the time 09:41 on the phones. |
| 2009 | **Bitcoin**<br>Bitcoin mining (creating new bitcoins and checking transactions) uses as much as energy as all the USA's fridges. |

# FA Cup Winners Since You Were Born

Many fans have waited decades to see their team lift the cup; many more are still waiting. Here are the teams that have hoisted the trophy in your lifetime (last win in brackets).

West Bromwich Albion ⚽ (1967-68)
Leeds United ⚽ (1971-72)
Sunderland ⚽ (1972-73)
Southampton ⚽ (1975-76)
Ipswich Town ⚽ (1977-78)
West Ham United ⚽ (1979-80)
Coventry City ⚽ (1986-87)
**Wimbledon** ⚽ (1987-88)

Wimbledon shocked the country in 1988 when they beat First Division champions Liverpool in the FA Cup final, overcoming 17-1 odds.

Tottenham Hotspur ⚽ (1990-91)
Everton ⚽ (1994-95)
Portsmouth ⚽ (2007-08)
Wigan Athletic ⚽ (2012-13)
Manchester United ⚽ (2015-16)
**Chelsea** ⚽ (2017-18)

Former Chelsea and Ivory Coast striker Didier Drogba is the only player to score in four separate FA Cup Finals.

Manchester City ⚽ (2018-19)
Arsenal ⚽ (2019-20)
**Leicester City** ⚽ (2020-21)

The Foxes first FA Cup was a long time coming – as was their first triumph in the Premier League, achieved in 2015/16. Faithful fans who laid bets at 5,000 to 1 at the start of that season were richly rewarded; others did the same but cashed out early, enticed by the bookies.

**Liverpool** ⚽ (2021-22)

Back in the final on a mission to avenge the loss a decade earlier to the same team, Chelsea. Liverpool took the match to win on penalties – just as they had when they lifted the cup in 2005-06, playing West Ham.

# Gameshow Hosts of the Seventies and Eighties

What do points make? I've started so I'll finish. Shut that door! You can't beat a bit of Bully! The catchphrases echo down the ages from these much-loved TV favourites.

David Vine ⋈ (A Question of Sport)
Stuart Hall ⋈ (It's a Knockout)
Anneka Rice ⋈ (Treasure Hunt)
Kenneth Kendall ⋈ (Treasure Hunt)
**Cilla Black** ⋈ (Blind Date)
Born Priscilla White, the stage name of Cilla Black came about by mistake. Featured in the first issue of Mersey Beat newspaper, the journalist accidentally called her Cilla Black. Cilla liked the name and opted to keep it.

Barry Cryer ⋈ (Jokers Wild)
Nicholas Parsons ⋈ (Just a Minute, Sale of the Century)
**Jim Bowen** ⋈ (Bullseye)
After completing his national service in the bomb disposal unit, Jim Bowen worked as a teacher and was promoted to deputy head, but gave up teaching once he appeared on The Comedians alongside Mike Reid.

Mike Read ⋈ (Pop Quiz)
David Coleman ⋈ (A Question of Sport)
Prof. Heinz Wolff ⋈ (The Great Egg Race)
Bob Holness ⋈ (Blockbusters)
Magnus Magnusson ⋈ (Mastermind)
Angela Rippon ⋈ (Masterteam)
**Noel Edmonds** ⋈ (Telly Addicts)
Noel Edmonds has made headlines for plotting to buy the BBC, starting a pet counselling service, and driving a mannequin called Candice around in his black cab to dissuade the public from trying to flag him down.

Ted Rogers ⋈ (3-2-1)
Terry Wogan ⋈ (Blankety Blank)
Les Dawson ⋈ (Blankety Blank)
Larry Grayson ⋈ (The Generation Game)

# Popular Food in the 1980s

Our last trolley dash takes us down the aisle at lunchtime, piled high with eat-on-the-go snacks and sandwiches. Stop on the way home for a deep pan pizza and a Diet Coke; end the day with a slice of Battenberg cake. Congratulations, you've just eaten the eighties!

### Crunchy Nut Cornflakes
The cereal was invented in Manchester in 1980. Pity the poor Americans: it took 30 years for Crunchy Nut to cross the Atlantic.

Kellogg's Fruit and Fibre

### Prepacked sandwiches
The prepacked sandwich was first sold by M&S in spring 1980. The range was small, conservative, made in-store and used whatever ingredients were plentiful (even if that was pilchards).

Viennetta

### Trifle
In 1596, Thomas Dawson recorded the first recipe for trifle in his books, *The Good Huswifes Jewell*. It was essentially thick cream, rosewater, sugar and ginger. Jelly didn't appear until the 1700s.

Chicken Kiev

Vol au vent

Battenberg cake

### Pizza
Pizza Hut claim to be the first company to sell food online – one of their signature pizzas via their Pizanet website, back in 1994.

Garlic bread

Kiwi

Sun-dried tomatoes

Potato waffles

Happy Meals

### Diet Coke
Within two years of its unveiling in 1982, Diet Coke became the most popular diet soft drink in the world, and the third most popular soft drink overall behind Coca Cola and Pepsi.

Rowntree's Drifters

Hedgehog-flavoured crisps

Burton's fish 'n' chips

Chicken satay

# Eighties Symbols of Success

In the flamboyant era of Dallas and Dynasty there were many ways to show that you, too, had really made it. Forty years on, it's fascinating to see how some of these throwbacks are outdated or available to nearly everyone, while others are still reserved for today's wealthy peacocks.

Car phone
Dishwasher
Children at private school

**Waterbed**
The modern-day waterbed was designed by a US student for his master's thesis project. Original fillings included corn syrup, and then jelly, before he settled on water. They were popular but problematic due to their weight and susceptibility to puncture, as Edward Scissorhands found out.

Second cars
Holidays abroad
Conservatory
Pony
Colour TV
Diamonds
Cordless phone

**Birkin bag**
A chance encounter between Hermès Executive Chairman Jean-Louis Dumas and Jane Birkin on a plane inspired the Birkin bag. The contents of Birkin's bag spilled out, and Dumas suggested she needed a bag with pockets, so Birkin sketched her idea on a sick bag.

Double glazing
Rolex watch
Leather Filofax
Mont Blanc pen

**Newton's Cradle desk toy**
Named after Isaac Newton and the cat's cradle, an early version was wooden, expensive and sold at Harrods. Chrome imitations followed. TV programme Myth Busters built a supersized cradle with concrete-filled chrome wrecking balls… it didn't work.

Stone cladding

The first UK car phone call was made in 1959 from outside the Lymm Hotel in Cheshire; human operators were used to connect calls until the 1980s. John Lennon wrote the lyrics for I'm Only Sleeping on the back of a car phone demand letter.

# Cars of the 1980s

Many cars you might associate with the eighties were on the road long before then, from the Ford Granada and Escort to the Porsche 911. But this is the decade they arguably hit their stride alongside other automotive icons.

**Toyota Corolla**
Introduced in 1966, the Toyota Corolla became the best-selling car worldwide by 1974. The car was named after a ring of petals.

Volvo 240

BMW 3 Series

**Volkswagen Golf**
Sold as the Rabbit in the US and the Caribe in Mexico.

Volkswagen Passat

Vauxhall Astra

Triumph Acclaim

**Porsche 911**
Originally the Porsche 901 on its 1964 debut, the name was changed after Peugeot claimed they had exclusive rights to naming cars with three digits and a zero in the middle.

Jaguar XJS

Nissan Micra

Peugeot 205

Austin Maestro

**Vauxhall Nova**
The Vauxhall Nova inspired a series of comical bumper stickers, including 'You've been Novataken', and 'Vauxhall Casanova'. It was called the Corsa everywhere but Britain where it sounded too much like the word 'coarser'. It was renamed anyway in 1993.

**Ford Sierra**
Neil Kinnock had one of the first Sierras. He wrecked it in a crash.

Austin Montego

Volkswagen Polo

**Austin Metro**
Promoted with comical adverts, the car became one of the best-selling cars in UK history, and even Princess Diana owned one.

**Ford Fiesta**
The Fiesta is the UK's best-selling car of all time.

Vauxhall Cavalier

# Eighties TV Gameshows

By the eighties, new formats aimed at youngsters – your youngsters? – were introduced. Some shows went digital or took to the skies; others kept it (very) simple, and a few remain family favourites to this day.

The Adventure Game

Treasure Hunt

**Blind Date**

The pilot episode of Blind Date was hosted by Duncan Norvelle, but he was quickly replaced by Cilla Black. Black presented the entire original run of the series for eighteen years, before unexpectedly announcing her departure on the show's first ever live episode.

Surprise Surprise

Countdown

Catchphrase

Blockbusters

Telly Addicts

**3-2-1**

The show's mascot and booby prize, Dusty Bin, cost around £10,000 to build. He was built by visual effects engineer Ian Rowley, who also operated Dusty Bin in the studio.

Blankety Blank

**Bob's Full House**

The instantly recognisable scoreboard was dubbed Mr Babbage by original host Bob Monkhouse. This was a nod to Charles Babbage, the inventor of the first programmable computer. In the reboot, Mr Babbage was replaced with a colour scoreboard, but the original board soon returned.

Bullseye

Cheggers Plays Pop

Family Fortunes

The Great Egg Race

Give Us a Clue

The Krypton Factor

Play Your Cards Right

The Price is Right

The Pyramid Game

# Popular Boys' Names

The most favoured names are now a curious blend of the evergreen (Thomas), rediscovered (Harry), and shorter names like Leo that echo past favourites (Leon, Leonard).

**Noah**

It's been a 20-year journey for Noah but at last he's made it to the top spot and toppled Oliver from his decade-long reign.

Oliver
George
Arthur
Muhammad
Leo
Harry
Oscar
Archie
Henry
Theodore
Freddie
Jack
Charlie
Theo
Alfie
Jacob
Thomas
Finley
Arlo
William
Lucas
Roman
Tommy
Isaac
Teddy
Alexander
Luca

**Rising stars:**

Brody is a new entrant to the Top 100 in 2021. So is Rupert who hasn't made the list before, even in the heyday of our yellow-trousered friend!

# Books of the Decade

Our final decade of books are the bookstore favourites from your fifties. How many did you read...and can you remember the plot, or the cover?

| | |
|---|---|
| 2013 | Doctor Sleep by Stephen King |
| 2014 | Big Little Lies by Liane Moriarty |
| 2015 | **The Girl on the Train by Paula Hawkins** |

The use of the word 'girl' in the title of the book sparked debate upon its release. It was speculated that it was used to liken it to Gone Girl, but it was used in the working title long before Hawkins had read Gone Girl.

| | |
|---|---|
| 2016 | Dark Matter by Blake Crouch |
| 2017 | Little Fires Everywhere by Celeste Ng |
| 2018 | Where the Crawdads Sing by Delia Owens |
| 2018 | **The Outsider by Stephen King** |

It's not unusual to see a character from one Stephen King novel appear in another. Before appearing in The Outsider, Holly Gibney had been a part of the Bill Hodges trilogy, and later the main character in If It Bleeds.

| | |
|---|---|
| 2019 | The Beekeeper of Aleppo by Christy Lefteri |
| 2019 | **The Silent Patient by Alex Michaelides** |

As a disillusioned screenwriter, Michaelides wrote a novel which became The Silent Patient. The story was inspired by the Greek heroine Alcestis.

| | |
|---|---|
| 2020 | The Vanishing Half by Brit Bennett |
| 2020 | The Midnight Library by Matt Haig |
| 2020 | The Thursday Murder Club by Richard Osman |
| 2020 | **Hamnet by Maggie O'Farrell** |

A fictionalised account of Hamnet, the real-life son of William Shakespeare who died in 1596 at the age of 11 – although the Bard is never mentioned by name.

| | |
|---|---|
| 2021 | The Wife Upstairs by Rachel Hawkins |
| 2021 | Klara and the Sun by Kazuo Ishiguro |
| 2021 | Beautiful World, Where Are You by Sally Rooney |
| 2021 | Are We Having Fun Yet? by Lucy Mangan |
| 2022 | It Starts With Us by Colleen Hoover |

April 17 1970: Jim Lovell is brought aboard a helicopter, the last of the
three astronauts from the Apollo 13 mission to be lifted from the floating

# Apollo Astronauts

Of those who have been to the moon, twelve landed, twelve remained in orbit. Gus Grissom, Ed White, and Roger B Chaffee died in training. BBC and ITV broadcast the June 1969 landing live in the first all-night transmission. Touchdown was at 9.17pm UK time – past your bedtime? – but Armstrong didn't take his monumental step until 3.56am.

*Landed on the moon:*
Alan Bean
**Alan Shepard**
Shepard was the oldest person to walk on the moon at the age of 47.

Buzz Aldrin
Charles Duke
David Scott
Edgar Mitchell
Eugene Cernan
Harrison Schmitt
James Irwin
John Young
Neil Armstrong
Pete Conrad
*Remained in low orbit:*
Al Worden
**Bill Anders**
Anders took the iconic Earthrise photo.

Dick Gordon
Frank Borman
Fred Haise
Jack Swigert
Jim Lovell
Ken Mattingly
Michael Collins
**Ron Evans**
Made the final spacewalk of the program to retrieve film cassettes.

**Stuart Roosa**
On the Apollo 14 mission he carried seeds from 5 species of trees. They were planted across the US and are known as Moon Trees.

Tom Stafford

# Popular Girls' Names

**58**

Of the fifty names that made the Top 10 from 1900-74, only four have appeared since: Claire, Emma, Samantha and Sarah. (Oddly, names beginning with 'D' are now a rarity with no Top 10 entries in the last fifty years!)

### Olivia
Along with other names ending in 'a' – look at the top five names here! – Olivia rose to popularity in the late nineties and has remained a favourite ever since. She's been number one or two from 2008 to the present day.

Amelia
Isla
Ava
Ivy
Freya
Lily
Florence
Mia
Willow
Rosie
Sophia
Isabella
Grace
Daisy
Sienna
Poppy
Elsie
Emily
Ella
Evelyn
Phoebe
Sofia
Evie
Charlotte

### Rising stars:
Unusually, we saw no new names in 2021 – although keep an eye on Maeve, climbing fast. Why? She's the on/off love interest of new boy Otis in the hit Netflix series Sex Education!

# Things People Did When You Were Growing Up (Part 2)

Finally, here are more of the things we saw, we did and errands we ran as kids that nobody needs, wants, or even understands how to do in the modern age!

✦ Drink syrup of figs
✦ Preserve vegetables
✦ Save the silver chocolate papers from Roses
✦ **Eat offal**
Tripe was never on ration but long out of favour by the time the tripe dresser's fate was sealed in 1992, when BSE broke out.

✦ **Make a carbon copy**
Carbon paper was first patented by Ralph Wedgwood, son of Thomas Wedgwood, in 1806, for his Noctograph – designed to help blind people write without ink. The smell and texture are just a memory, but emails sent in 'cc' (carbon copy) might remind you!

✦ **Wash handkerchiefs**
You'd have to keep (and wash) a hanky for nine years to outweigh the $CO_2$ emissions of its tissue cousins.

✦ Use talcum powder
✦ Make a penfriend
✦ **Wire a plug**
Strip and route wires to the terminal; fit the right fuse. Not any more. In 1994, it became illegal to sell appliances without fitted plugs.

✦ Darn a hole in your sock
✦ Refill your pen from an inkwell
✦ Wind on your camera for another shot
✦ See the bones in your foot at the shoe shop through a Pedoscope
✦ Pluck a chicken
✦ **Smoke on a bus**
'When will this fanaticism going to stop?' asked one MP in 1962, about a proposed ban on lower-deck smoking.

✦ Scrape ice patterns off the inside of your bedroom window
✦ Service your own car
✦ Buy starch or blue bags for your washing
✦ **Play Spot the Ball**
Spot the Ball was launched in 1973. More than 10 years passed without a jackpot winner as its popularity declined.

Printed in Great Britain
by Amazon

27652124R10058